FORD FIESTA

MARK BRADBURY

AMBERLEY

Front cover: The first ST, based on the fifth generation Fiesta with a 148-bhp, 2.0-litre DOHC Duratec. (Ford)

Back cover: The Finnish combo of Mikko Hirvonen and Jarmo Lehtinen in a Ford Fiesta World Rally Championship (WRC) RS on their way to an outright win in the 2011 Rally of Sweden. (Graham Robson Collection)

First published 2025

Amberley Publishing
The Hill, Stroud,
Gloucestershire, GL5 4EP

www.amberley-books.com

ISBN: 978 1 3981 2383 0 (print)
ISBN: 978 1 3981 2384 7 (ebook)

British Library Cataloguing in Publication Data.
A catalogue record for this book is available from the British Library.

Typeset in 10pt on 13pt Celeste.
Typesetting by SJmagic DESIGN SERVICES, India.
Printed in the UK.

Appointed GPSR EU Representative: Easy Access System Europe Oü, 16879218
Address: Mustamäe tee 50, 10621, Tallinn, Estonia
Contact Details: gpsr.requests@easproject.com, +358 40 500 3575

Contents

Acknowledgements

Thanks must go to a group of my friends who have checked and commented on the manuscript several times with unstinting enthusiasm: motoring journalist Malcolm Bobbitt, curator of the British Motor Museum Cat Boxall and her assistant curator Amy Forster-Smith, former Ford employee Lawrence Thomas and automotive engineer Jonathan Wankling. I'm also grateful to Nick Hull and David Burgess-Wise for their wise words and help with some of the images.

Apart from the photos that are clearly attributed and those that I have taken myself of various friends' and acquaintances' cars (many thanks), I would like to thank Len Keen and Chris Smith from the Ford of Britain Heritage Collection at Daventry for the unfettered access to the cars in their care. Gratitude also has to go to author and historian John Nikas for providing images from the collection of the late Graham Robson which he now has in his possession, and for his contacts in Ford HQ at Dearborn which eased the access to the Ford press and previously published images.

Most books require research from a variety of sources. This book would have been very difficult to write without a publication by the late Edouard Seidler entitled *Let's Call it Fiesta,* with the very apt subtitle *The Auto-biography of Ford's Project Bobcat.* Unusually, Seidler was invited by Ford to follow the design and development of the Fiesta during the three or four years prior to the car's launch in 1976, and then publish the results in a book (it was available within days of the car's unveiling). Very little was off-limits to Seidler; on a daily basis he was invited to a wide variety of meetings, design studios and focus groups, and the firm's photographers were at his disposal. In his last paragraph, Seidler suggests that his title tells the story of the *birth* of the Fiesta; this book covers a similar phase but also relates the car's formative years, its middle age, its sporting achievements and, finally, its retirement.

Yet again and last but by no means least, my long-suffering wife Jill must also be thanked. Apart from it being her suggestion to write this book, Jill has helped me take and select images, and has had to endure far too much Ford chatter over the past few months.

Mark Bradbury

Introduction

On 25 October 2022, the Ford Motor Company announced that production of the Ford Fiesta was planned to end, and on Friday 7 July the following year, the last two examples rolled off from the one remaining set of Fiesta production lines in Cologne, Germany. That final pair of Fiestas were to stay with Ford. Signed by every member of the team who worked on the cars, one was set to join the firm's international heritage fleet in the city where it was built, and the other would be shipped to the Ford of Britain Heritage Collection in Daventry, Northamptonshire.

The star of the show! A first generation 1981 Ford Fiesta 997cc Popular Plus finished in Dove Grey. Notice the period-correct number plates, tax disc and Feu Orange air freshener dangling from the mirror – all part of the attention to detail many owners have. The driving lamps are a relatively recent addition by a former keeper. (Author)

Over a century ago, Henry Ford established several ground-breaking ideas and philosophies that would lead to the global mobility many of us enjoy today, and he paved the way for many other motor manufacturers to follow. This book describes the background of Ford in Europe before explaining the need for a small car in the late 1960s, and then detailing the design, launch and onward development of the Bobcat project, or the Ford Fiesta, as it is much better known.

The Fiesta became a car loved by millions; it is still enthusiastically owned, driven, adored and admired today despite the end of its production after forty-seven years and seven versions.

1

Ford in Europe – The Background

As will become clear as this story unfolds, the Ford Fiesta of 1976 was as important and as revolutionary for the Ford Motor Company as the Model T had been for motoring nearly seventy years before it. Unlike the rich person's expensive playthings from other manufacturers, the Model T was designed from the outset to be inexpensive and robust as well as easy to drive and maintain. With demand exceeding supply in the early years, the founder of the firm, Henry Ford, devised ground-breaking production-line methods to produce many more cars at an increasingly lower price; it was the runaway success of the Model T that led to the expansion of the Ford Motor Company into various other countries, including Great Britain and most of Europe. After building over 15 million Model Ts, as well as many other top-selling successors, Ford became one of the world's greatest motor manufacturers.

Henry Ford (1863–1947), founder of the Ford Motor Company, standing beside the masterpiece that started mass production in motor cars, the Ford Model T. Ford is pictured here with one of the just over 15 million produced. (Ford)

Ford in Europe

The expansion of Henry Ford's empire after the end of the First World War was dramatic. With Ford's Highland Park factory in Michigan in the US nearing capacity, the giant River Rouge plant was opened in 1928 at nearby Dearborn. It was a new type of all-in-one factory: it took raw materials such as ore and coke directly off ships, generated its own power, cast its engine and transmission casings, built vehicles and shipped them by either road or water just a few hours later. Ford vehicles were selling well not just in the US but in many other countries, including parts of Europe, and Henry Ford knew that to adopt his methods of production elsewhere, 'The Rouge' needed to be the blueprint for other sites, and what better place to start than Britain, and then Germany – the two prime markets at that time.

The existing Ford factories in Britain and Germany – Trafford Park in Manchester and a similar site on the outskirts of Berlin – were at capacity producing the Model T and its successor the A, and both were deemed unsuitable for expansion along the lines Henry envisaged. After much searching, nearly 500 acres of the north bank of the River Thames in Essex were purchased, and work began on the new site in May 1929. Two years later, the Ford Motor Company Ltd opened Dagenham, the biggest car plant in Europe at that time. Spurred on by the purchase of a majority share of Germany's biggest exporter of cars,

Henry Ford's grandson Henry Ford II (1917–87), 'HFII', took over the reins of the family firm in 1947. HFII supported the development of many models in the Ford range and he was a leading light in the desire for the company to produce a new small car. That car would eventually be launched as the Ford Fiesta. (Ford)

Opel, by arch-rival General Motors (GM) in 1929, Henry Ford made his next move. With a pledge to build a large ore-to-car plant in Germany like those in the US and now in Britain, the mayor of Cologne, Konrad Adenauer, eased the way for Ford to build a similar facility in his city. Ideally sited alongside a large, sea-bound river, the first German-built Ford, a Model A-based truck built using many locally made parts, rolled off the Cologne production lines in May 1931. By the establishment of these large, mass-production, all-in-one factories, Ford could now compete for the European market alongside GM (which had also snapped up the by then struggling Vauxhall Motors in Britain).

With the main European Ford factories located in Britain and Germany, albeit with several smaller satellite plants spread across the Continent, several ranges of similar but not identical vehicles had been developed, leading to unnecessary production proliferation and the attendant inefficiency. In 1967, Detroit merged all European operations into a new and local subsidiary. One of the primary objectives of the new 'Ford of Europe' division was to remove duplicity by rationalising vehicle ranges into one to suit all markets. Initially managed by Dagenham, the Continental automobile market eclipsed that in Britain and, by the end of the 1990s, new car development and the headquarters had moved to Cologne.

The Ford Motor Company went public in 1956, but the Ford family retained 40 per cent of the voting rights. Henry Ford died on 7 April 1947, aged eighty-three, and didn't see the success of the company after the Second World War, but his grandson Henry Ford II (born in 1917 and known throughout Ford as HFII) was CEO during the design and development of several Ford products including the much-loved Fiesta.

Ford Today

The automotive landscape has changed dramatically since Henry Ford built his first car, yet the Ford Motor Company remains one of the world's most important manufacturers. It took Ford nearly twenty years to build a million cars but, in 2023 alone, 4.4 million vehicles were produced worldwide with 177,000 employees returning a net income of $4.33 billion. Ford's manufacturing operations are truly international and include sites in North and South America, China, India, Australia, South Africa and many countries in Europe.

Production of cars ceased in Britain in 2002, but Ford continued to manufacture diesel engines in Dagenham and transmissions in Halewood, Merseyside. Ford Dunton in Essex was opened in 1967, and it was assigned responsibility within Ford of Europe for various aspects of vehicle design with a particular focus on interiors, and this is still the case. With technical innovation becoming increasingly vital in the automotive world, the Ford site is now also home to the Dunton Campus, a major automotive research and development facility with several thousand staff working alongside their colleagues at the Merkenich Technical Centre in Cologne. Dunton is also the headquarters of the UK division of Ford Motor Credit Company and home to the company's UK sales and marketing departments.

Dearborn – where the Ford story began – will always be inextricably linked to the Ford Motor Company. It remains home to the mighty River Rouge plant, but also houses the company's headquarters at the Henry Ford II World Center. With the need to maintain its position in the hierarchy of motor manufacturers, work has also started on transforming the former Research and Engineering Centre into the Dearborn Campus which, like its European counterparts, will become the US home to thousands of Ford designers, engineers and product development staff.

Ford has moved with the times and saloon cars have largely been replaced by the SUV and the crossover. Commercial vehicles still feature very strongly with the best-selling Ford being the F-150 pickup truck. First appearing in the US in 1948, the F-Series is now on the fourteenth version and, in 2023 alone, nearly 750,000 were sold – more than one for every minute of the year.

At the time of writing, the executive chairman of the Ford Motor Company is William Clay Ford Junior – the great-grandson of founder Henry Ford – with Jim Farley as president and chief executive officer (CEO).

2

The Need for a Small Ford

In 1959, the British Motor Corporation (BMC) took the motoring world by surprise and launched the Austin Mini Seven and the Morris Mini-Minor, two variants of the same car just with different badges and radiator grilles. Designed by Alec Issigonis, the diminutive Mini – it was just a whisker over 10 feet long – was a masterpiece of packaging and technical achievements. With its transverse engine driving the front wheels and seating for four, it made the other two recently launched competitors, the Triumph Herald and the Ford Anglia 105E, seem very ordinary and soon looked outdated. The Mini retained its freshness right through the 1960s, and appealed to all types of owners from students and newly qualified drivers to film stars and pop musicians; the Mini coincided with the fashion and political statements of the time, and became *the* car to be seen in. The Model T may have been voted the most influential car of the twentieth century, but it was the Mini that came second, such was its significance.

Before the arrival of the Mini, Ford in the US was adamant that family cars were where the profit was and that there would be no money to be made from producing small cars, but the Mini changed the plans of many manufacturers. Ford was one of the first companies to become adept at both product planning and detailed cost analysis to the point of them becoming a science; the former ensures that the right product is built at the right time, and the latter makes sure the cost of producing that product remains under very tight control – down to the last cent. Ford obtained an example of the Mini, performed a complete strip-down and established that the Mini would cost £5 (GBP) more to build than an Anglia, yet it was priced at £30 *less*, so the conclusion was that the Mini was being produced at a loss. Despite this analysis and the company's previous misgivings, Ford management decided that, properly engineered and built efficiently, a small car *could* be profitable and, as the 1960s progressed, it became clear to most car manufacturers (particularly those in Europe) that there was sufficient demand for such cars. These firms also knew that to attract customers away from the Mini, any new car in Class B (the industry's designation for small cars) had to be significantly better than the BMC offering.

The post-war era saw great social change. With both partners working, families often became two-car households, and it was accepted that along with one main family car, the other could be smaller and more economical. With better-paid jobs available, an increasing number

It was the BMC Mini that really set the cat among the pigeons! Built by apprentices for motor shows, this sectioned version demonstrates what a packaging masterpiece Alec Issigonis had created. Left-hand drive not only pandered to European buyers, but conveniently left most of the interesting parts on display. (James Mann/© British Motor Industry Heritage Trust)

of new drivers could afford a car, and, for their first car, they usually chose something smaller – often the same type they had learnt in. BMC already had the A30, later the A35 and then the Mini, and many other companies had a range of models to cover a family's requirements. Ford could offer them the family car but not the second car, or even the new driver's first car; since the larger Fords were less appealing to these buyers, its global market share suffered. The company needed to expand their range into the burgeoning small car arena and, despite the view that smaller profits might be the result, it was keen to take on the challenge.

The Class B Market

Another reason Ford wanted to produce a Class B car – the smallest ever to be produced by the company up to that point – was European market penetration, or lack of it. In 1970, Ford had 26.6 per cent in the UK, 14.7 per cent in (West) Germany, 13.3 per cent in Belgium and 12 per cent in the Netherlands. Ford's share in France and Italy (the prime areas for small cars largely due to a favourable taxation system for less powerful engines) was less than 5 per cent, and with very tough import restrictions of no more than 250 vehicles per year, the market in Spain for foreign manufacturers was practically zero. During the 1960s, Spain was viewed as one of the principal expansion areas in Europe. Such was the pace of change on the Iberian Peninsula in the decades after the fall-out from the Spanish Civil War, it was forecast that its small car sales, with its taxation advantages similar to those in France and Italy, would amount to a million cars by the 1980s, and HFII was keen not to be left out.

Despite starting from nowhere in 1969, Ford's experts forecast that developing a successful small car might provide the firm with around 13 per cent of the European Class B market by 1980. With such enticing figures, both HFII and Lee Iacocca (president of the Ford Motor Company from 1969), encouraged Ford of Europe to build a small car, positioned beneath the Escort. Little did anyone know then that in October 1973 there would be an oil crisis, precipitated by the temporary cessation of oil shipments from the Middle East to the US and other countries in retaliation for the support of Israel during the Yom Kippur War. Fuel prices doubled overnight. The situation was relieved in March 1974, but the chance of a repeat frightened many drivers into more economical cars. With a car set to cost the European motorist 40 per cent more by 1975, and ownership of small cars expected to rise by over 5 per cent, a move by Ford into Class B was almost perfectly timed.

Lido Anthony 'Lee' Iacocca (1924–2019) joined Ford in 1946 and rose to president in 1970. He is often considered to be the father of the Mustang, but he was also instrumental in the development of other models, including the Ford Fiesta. A failed attempt by Iacocca to usurp HFII led to him being fired in 1978. (Ford)

Other Manufacturers

During the late 1960s, rumours circulated about new small cars being developed by Fiat and Renault, and in 1971, the Fiat 127 was launched as the first real rival for the Mini. Initially only available with a boot, a hatchback version appeared the following year and that configuration soon became the norm. It was a successful car and, despite being slightly boxy and slab-sided, it sold well throughout Europe and Britain, and was voted European Car of the Year in 1971. The Renault 5 appeared a few months later in January of the following year, and its styling was a revelation; it was gently curvaceous, flowing and looked unlike anything else on the market with its smooth, body-contoured plastic bumpers. The Fiat, however, was the starting point for the new small Ford; stylish and chic though the R5 was, its engine and gearbox were arranged longitudinally and they encroached on the cabin. Despite the better looks of the French car, the transverse engine of the 127 provided more interior space. Ford knew it wasn't the Mini it had to beat, or even the Renault 5, it was the Fiat 127.

Stylish and chic, though flawed in terms of mechanical packaging with its longitudinally mounted engine, the Renault 5 was launched in 1972 and soon became the best-selling car in France. (Author)

The Fiat 127 was launched in 1971 and, with its transverse engine, was considered to be the car to beat. During the development of the Fiesta, the 127 would also serve as a convenient development mule for the Ford and it was unlikely to attract prying eyes. (Fiat)

3

Project Bobcat

In the closing months of 1969, Ford finally made a top-level decision to start work on a Class B car and, in January 1970, an initial set of cost and weight targets was produced. Ford's product planners set some firm goals: the new car had to cost $100 less than the Escort (just over £1,000 today), weigh no more than 1,400 lb (630 kg) and, with Ford being one of the last manufacturers to break into the small car market, it had to be significantly better than the competition. Later that year, a concept car was completed for showing at the design studios at Merkenich in Cologne, Germany. In February 1971, following some extra work, mock-ups and various design sketches were shown to HFII and Iacocca at the Dunton design studio in Essex, England. HFII was keen for Ford of Europe to lead the project, but its designers and engineers were fully occupied working on the Mk2 Escort and the Capri II, as well as the replacement for the Mk4 Zephyr and Zodiac. With other manufacturers already producing potential competitors, in September 1972 the design studios at Dearborn took the lead. In the meantime, competing cars including the Renault 5, the Fiat 127, the Datsun Cherry, the Honda Civic, the BMC Mini and even Ford's own Escort as a baseline were stripped down to the last nut and bolt for a detailed cost analysis to be performed, and to set targets for the new model; the process was almost certainly a crib too, to see what made the competitors' cars tick.

Mini-Mite and the Blue Car

Suspecting that front-wheel drive was the best solution but being unsure, the development team at Dearborn decided to build two prototypes. Called Mini-Mite, one was based on a cut-down rear-wheel-drive Escort, and a second used the front-wheel-drive underpinnings from a Fiat 127 – simply a convenient donor – and would allow a back-to-back comparison to be carried out. Ford was understandably a little wary of the newfangled front-wheel drive following the less than successful Taunus 12M launched in Germany in 1962, and the American Thunderbird prototype of the year before. Both cars were expensive to develop and the Taunus was costly to manufacture, so the Thunderbird reverted to the tried and trusted rear-wheel-drive before it reached production. The Taunus made it through to the showrooms but it was unreliable and, with a buying public remaining suspicious of anything deemed unconventional, it didn't sell as well as planned. Feeling a little out of their depth with small cars, Dearborn commissioned the Italian design company Carrozzeria Ghia in Turin to produce a third car for comparison purposes. Known as the Blue Car, the Italian proposal was designed by Paolo Martin in just fifty-three days, and it too was based on the Fiat. In 1970, Ford bought a majority shareholding in Ghia, and during the following few years the studio became an integral part of Ford of Europe's styling operation.

One of the Mini-Mite prototypes built by Ford's design studio at Dearborn. This one is based on a cut-down rear-wheel-drive Ford Escort and was to help convince management and engineers alike that front-wheel drive was the preferred method of propulsion. (Ford)

The front-wheel-drive Mini-Mite prototype built by Ford at Dearborn. The eagle-eyed might be able to spot the Fiat 127 wheels which confirm that the underpinnings came from the small Italian. (Ford)

In 1962, Ford of Germany launched the third generation Taunus 12M. It shared some styling cues with the British Cortina, but underneath it had a V4 engine and it was the first front-wheel drive European Ford. Unfortunately, and despite the happy demeanour of the dog-walking couple here, it was not blessed with the usual Ford reliability. (Ford)

At the end of 1972, these three running prototypes were transported to Lausanne in Switzerland for evaluation by focus groups, or clinics, as they are sometimes called. During the course of a fortnight, 700 people from various walks of life were flown in from all over Europe and asked to compare the three cars against the usual competition. The list included the 127, Civic, R5, the recently launched Peugeot 104 and finally a Ford Escort, the latter as a reference point. All the vehicles presented were finished in the same colour to remove any subconscious decision based purely on aesthetics. To ensure a less Europe-specific response, and to emphasise the international aspirations for the new car, in early 1973, further sessions were held in California and São Paulo, Brazil. The public tested all three prototypes; the front-wheel-drive cars were the clear winners, and the size of the proposed new model was judged to be right for all European markets. It was no surprise that front-wheel drive won the day; more and more small cars were adopting the system and when various Ford engineers and management drove the Fiat, they started to consider the choice more seriously. It did, however, mean that development costs would increase; they would need a completely new drivetrain, a new plant to build it in and the finished product would have to be more expensive to recoup the investment. It had been forecast in *Motor* magazine in the mid-1970s that front-wheel drive and transverse engines would become the conventional mechanical layout, certainly for European cars, adding that it was perhaps the ultimate tribute to Alec Issigonis. It wasn't long before Iacocca decided he needed help with the European side of his responsibilities – particularly given that more engineering development would be required than had originally been envisaged – so he appointed Hal Sperlich, a well-respected product planner at Ford, as his 'Special Assistant'. Sperlich formed a link at an executive level between Ford US and Ford of Europe and one of his first successes – albeit a rather minor one – was christening the new small car project 'Bobcat'.

To explore alternatives to the US Mini-Mites, Ford's Italian design studio Ghia in Turin was employed to produce a running prototype. Imaginatively named the 'Blue Car' and based on the front-wheel-drive Fiat 127, it was designed by Paolo Martin in double-quick time. This car formed the basis of the first true Bobcat prototypes. (Ford)

Proving the Concept

With an urgency to move Bobcat into development and eventually production, Ford management pushed for a design freeze and Iacocca told Sperlich he needed Dearborn to produce a running prototype by June 1973. Five were created: four used Fiat 127 bodies with Ford specifics (front suspension on one, rear on another, a complete drivetrain on a third and a fourth with heating, ventilation and electrics); the fifth was pure Ford, combining all four features, and it represented the prototype as requested. Most manufacturers use 'mules' (the four 127-bodied prototypes in Ford's case), allowing the various sub-assemblies to be tested and developed individually, at reduced cost and, if necessary, in secret.

In the meantime, in April 1973, Tom Tjaarda, the American design director at Ghia and responsible for many designs including the De Tomaso Pantera and the Ferrari 365 Californian, took the Blue Car to his studio had created, and produced two more versions. Both named Wolf, one had an extended roof line to create rear luggage space, and the other was a two-door saloon with a sloping roof to the rear. Ford's top management at

The Blue Car was a good start, but Paolo Martin's colleague at Ghia, Tom Tjaarda, thought it could be even better. He created two versions known as 'Wolf': a saloon (seen here and the one preferred by Dearborn) and a small estate car. The Wolf saloon was to have a major impact on the design trajectory of the Bobcat project. (Ford)

Dearborn preferred these studies to their own – especially the saloon version. The saloon was a running prototype with a Kent engine (from the Escort), and among the first to drive it on the Dearborn test track were HFII and Lee Iacocca. With the competitors' cars available for comparison, they were both impressed with the Bobcat prototype.

Ford of Europe Get Involved

In mid-1973, the design teams at Dunton and Merkenich completed their backlog. Ford of Europe were keen that it should have significant input in their new Class B car, so Phil Caldwell (chairman of the European operation) who had gleaned that Dearborn felt uncomfortable working with small cars, asked HFII to send the Bobcat project to Europe. Ford of Europe had collaborated with the project all along and were very familiar with it, so it wouldn't take long to start work. Uwe Bahnsen, a designer at Ford in Germany who would later rise to vice president of design for Ford of Europe, and Jack Telnack, his British counterpart who was to become Ford's global vice president of design, took the Wolf prototype as a starting point. Their design teams combined it with design cues from the Capri II and the Mk2 Escort such as the side flutes and angular detail – gone were the rounded features of some of the American studies. Two-dimensional, 2- or 3-inch-thick plywood mock-ups, painted, glazed and fitted with just two wheels, provided a quick-to-implement, economical but very effective method of presenting ideas. Having met the deadline of the product planning committee meeting at Merkenich on 21 June 1973, it was agreed that the styling should be based on the saloon version of the Ghia Wolf, but with the side profiles

Above: The Merkenich view of how project Bobcat should look. One can start to see the eventual design of the Fiesta, particularly in the side profile with the swooping line of the door and the shape of the rear side window. Note the outline of a Bobcat on the grille. (Ford)

Below: The rear view of the Merkenich design. The fuel filler is in the final position for a Fiesta, yet the door 'handles' are much like those on the Renault 5. It has a stylised 'Bobcat' script on the boot lid, but the lid is just that; the hatchback had not yet appeared. (Ford)

modified in line with those presented by Ford of Europe. To eke out as much as possible in terms of additional ideas and suggestions from both Dunton and Merkenich, the two teams were encouraged to produce their own individual variations.

More Clinics

Further rounds of customer clinics were held to make quite sure that the proposed format of the Bobcat was what potential buyers might want. From across Europe, 7,000 buyers were interviewed in their homes, the results of which established that sales of the Escort would only be slightly affected by the Bobcat, and that two doors and a hatch would be preferred – several other mechanical details were also confirmed during these sessions. The demographic of the buyer was also considered: gender, status, age, income and so on; it became clear that in many markets, the Bobcat would be either a new driver's first car, or a family's second car. In another round of focus groups it was also established that front-wheel drive was indeed essential.

Another market-research exercise with 350 potential buyers in Germany and France, followed by clinics at Dunton, established interior preferences. Visibility, instrument layout, headroom, the size and accessibility of the boot and even the design of the door cards were presented, and useful feedback gained. Other group sessions led to the conclusion that 13 per cent of Bobcat buyers would eventually move up to another Ford model, whereas they would have bought something else if their first car had been another make – brand loyalty was, and remains, very important.

Final Selection and Formal Project Launch

Although many Ford personnel knew that a new car was being designed and developed, the internal launch was held on 2 October 1973. Following a brief introduction by HFII to the 150 Ford staff gathered in the ballroom of the Intercontinental Hotel in Cologne, Iacocca took to the podium to talk to the team responsible for the new car. With one of the latest Bobcat prototypes (one of the final, full-sized British models, in fact) sent to Merkenich in late 1973 and transferred under a cloak of secrecy to be alongside him on the stage, Iacocca reminded them that just 1,049 days remained before the first car would have to roll off the production line. He underlined the importance of the Bobcat by telling them about the predicted sales and that, until that first car appeared, the company would be spending $600,000 per day on Project Bobcat – *excluding* the cost of new factories.

The next day, 3 October, Merkenich hosted another product planning committee meeting, but this one was different; it would be at this meeting that the final design for Bobcat would be selected by ballot. This was the first time in the history of Ford that the process was democratic; the final choice of what to build and take to market was usually an executive decision. With the possibility of a last-minute reversion to any of the designs created so far, Dearborn, Turin, Dunton and Merkenich provided input, and four clay mock-ups and five fibreglass models were submitted for scrutiny. The competition was fierce, with every styling studio keen to get their design chosen. The choice was quickly narrowed down to the two from Ford of Europe:

With any new car there are very few items that don't require designing and modelling – even the smallest things. Here, a model of just one of several Bobcat steering wheel proposals is being completed using clay. (Hull/Ford)

the one from Dunton and the one from Merkenich – although the basic design of course was that from Tom Tjaarda at Ghia. After the fifteen senior Ford figures had examined every styling prototype minutely, they each cast their vote. With just one vote between them, the result was very close. In his book *Let's Call it Fiesta,* Edouard Seidler (who was present at the meeting) reports that Dunton were the victors, but Steve Saxty in his book *Secret Fords,* states they lost to Merkenich. Nick Hull in *Ford Design in the UK* agrees with Seidler but takes a more diplomatic view; he documents (and has since reaffirmed) that Jack Telnack's team at Dunton initially corrected a few aspects of the Ghia model, before the final work was performed by the *joint* efforts of both design studios, each team concentrating on their areas of expertise.

The demarcation between the German and British design teams was amicable but also a matter of pragmatism. At the time, Merkenich had better facilities for body styling and they took the lead on the exterior leaving Dunton solely responsible for the interior design. In reality, both teams, along with input from Turin, were involved, but an association with Germany was deemed an advantage; in the early 1970s, the UK motor industry suffered from quality and workforce issues, and, coupled with a view that Teutonic design was more progressive, Ford's marketing team decided that promoting the Bobcat as a crisp, German design would do no harm. Styling done, the Bobcat now had to be engineered, developed and tested – these items would be down to the Europeans working as a team.

Ford's facility at Merkenich in Germany in 1974, and the final exterior design for the Bobcat is being modelled using clay. The bridge structure slides and allows precise measurements of models to be recorded. Some of the competition can be seen in the background. (Hull/Ford)

Fibreglass was used to build both see-through models and low-cost styling mock-ups. This is Dunton but it's unclear whether this process led to the clear-panelled Fiesta being photographed at the British car body manufacturing plant Pressed Steel by a British Leyland Cowley photographer, and published later in this book. (Hull/Ford)

4

Engineering Underway

The team at Dearborn had done some work on an embryonic front-wheel-drive system needed for the Bobcat and had built a running prototype, but a European joint venture between the engineers at Merkenich and Dunton decided it would be best to start afresh. Having dismantled many competitors' cars and used several Fiat 127s as donors, as much was gained about how to do it as how *not* to do it. The original intention was that Bobcat would use the Kent engine from the Escort but, at 1,098 cc, the smallest was too large for taxation purposes in European countries and the block length was on the limit for transverse mounting (the only orientation considered). Therefore, to achieve a tax-friendly size of less than 1.0 litre, Ford's engineers reduced the bore by 7 mm, at the same time saving just over an inch in length (4 × 7 = 28 mm). Not only was it now suitably compact, but the 'new' engine was lighter and the stubbier crankshaft was stiff enough to run in three main bearings instead of five reducing frictional losses, one of the enemies of fuel consumption. Apart from the initial 957 cc unit created, a longer-stroke 1,117 cc version was produced for other markets. Further weight savings were made by casting the all-new front-wheel-drive transmission casing in aluminium alloy, although cast iron was retained for the engine. With a new engine, gearbox and final drive now being required, it became clear that the existing factories would not be able to cope with the predicted production figures.

Prototypes of the Bobcat

Despite the styling creations being referred to as prototypes, they were barely more than mock-ups. With the general styling finalised, the engineers could get immersed in producing prototype vehicles to prove that the resulting car could be built within the budget constraints and timescales, and that it performed as intended. Prototype vehicles often comprise only certain elements and the testing programme is carefully conceived to ensure that the appropriate prototype is available for a specific aspect of testing and proving.

One source suggests fourteen vehicles were built to accommodate an exhaustive test process, along with four others for crash testing, although Ford told the press in late 1976 that thirty-five engineering prototypes were built. Regardless of the numbers, they

Above: Finally looking like the first generation of Fiesta! This is the pale-blue, first mechanical prototype of the Bobcat – Prototype Number One. This car was deliberately written off as part of the crash testing programme but not before HFII and Iacocca were able to drive it. Vehicle historians all over the world must be very upset that this one wasn't tucked away and kept for posterity. (Ford)

Below: Various destructive tests are performed. This one verifies what happens when the car hits a solid object. The check pattern allows frame-by-frame analysis of the deceleration and deformation using high-speed filming techniques, and the brightly coloured front wheel and tyre makes them stand out as a reference; the numbers are part of the test-logging process. (Ford)

were built by hand at a cost of around $100,000 each and none have survived. Depending upon the tests, some vehicles were incomplete but representative – for example, frontal crash testing remained valid even if the rear of the car was simply a mock-up. Some were mechanical prototypes, comprising the Bobcat floorpan with Ford's engine, transmission, suspension, steering and brakes, but fitted with a Fiat 127 body. Perfectly adequate for verifying the running gear and with the need to tot up extensive distances in all climates, conditions and countries, the 127 shell provided a suitable disguise against prying eyes – they were also quicker and less expensive to build. Some competitors' cars were stripped of certain components, heaters and instruments for example, and fitted with the Bobcat equivalents. Ford of Europe bought at least thirty-three Fiat 127s, five Renault 5s, four Volkswagen Golfs, a brace of Polos and a solitary Peugeot 104 to help with their testing and development. About half of these purchases ended up destroyed in crash tests, sometimes in conjunction with the new Ford to check car-on-car collision performance.

Interior Comfort

As well as the general design, switch and control positions, Dunton considered every aspect of interior comfort but especially that of the driver. Using a 'package buck' – a mocked-up but dimensionally accurate and adjustable passenger compartment – they invited subjects from within Ford to get themselves comfortable in the driver's seat. Dozens of employees with various body shapes took part, and their preferred seating, pedal and steering wheel positions were logged. The aim was to try people of varying heights, leg lengths and so on, which corresponded to the middle 90 per cent distribution of the (European) population; the results were analysed by ergonomic specialists, and a range of suitable seat adjustments provided. The latest materials and fabrics were chosen for a smart, restful interior and submitted every few weeks to the fit and finish committee before being unleashed on more focus groups or customer clinics.

Prototype Sign-off

One of the Bobcat prototypes was selected to be the one that the executives would agree was the final design – except for alterations deemed necessary following testing – and would be signed off for the next phase of development. On 6 November 1974, HFII, Lee Iacocca and more than a dozen vice presidents arrived from Detroit to join the European engineers in driving the new car. Having been given one year to produce a running prototype, the engineering teams completed it in less than eleven months. The pale-blue car HFII and Iacocca were to drive, Bobcat Prototype Number One, had taken two months to build from hand-made panels and it was finished a little over a week before their visit. To avoid information leaks – there had been some from the clinics – the tests were staged at the carefully guarded test track at Dunton. Alongside the new Ford were most of its eventual competitors' cars to allow a true comparison to be made, and each driver was accompanied by a member of the Bobcat engineering team armed with a tape recorder and notepad to log any comments. The Bobcat wasn't perfect of course but it was very

It's 6 November 1974, and here's the pale-blue Bobcat Prototype Number One with an array of Ford executives – including HFII and Lee Iacocca – looking on. After they drove the car, it was confirmed that the development programme should continue in earnest. (Ford)

impressive. Following the session, the list of modifications was extensive but none were insurmountable: transmission noise (the car had minimal soundproofing), the seats were too hard, their adjustment mechanism was difficult to reach, the gearchange was stiff and so on – even the sun visors came in for comment. Despite the gripes, most of which were fully expected by the engineers with a relatively early prototype, the car was declared to be 'great' by HFII, and development and testing of the Bobcat was cleared to continue.

Testing

Ford management were keen that the development and testing process not only verified that the new car met its design requirements, but that it was *better* than the competition – hence the many other manufacturers' cars that were driven, dismantled, costed and crashed. The weight of the finished car was another area which attracted close attention. Unnecessary weight not only impacts performance, fuel consumption and handling, but also cost. Ford's production engineers spent months analysing every component, down to the last ounce, to see if anything could be reduced or deleted for production without compromising the car. Another area of concern was customer-perceived quality. The paint finish, the interior materials, the driving position and even the feel of the controls were all checked to make sure that the Bobcat was not lacking. Cost of ownership was also a top priority; making the car reliable, minimising the cost and amount of regular maintenance would be key. As an example, the body styling, with its various break lines (joins, physical or aesthetic), meant that, in the event of minor damage, only a small area would need attention thus helping to achieve a low insurance rating.

The testing phase relies on static and dynamic tests. The static test rigs at Merkenich were used to relentlessly exercise certain parts of the car from the window, door and boot controls, through the passenger seating to the suspension; the site also had environmental chambers to simulate weather extremes. The aim is to condense several years of ownership into just a matter of months – often to destruction – to find any weak points or areas needing improvement. Dynamic testing was carried out in secrecy at the 547-acre Ford proving ground at Lommel in Belgium, where Bobcats were driven at a variety of speeds and for many thousands of miles on its 17 miles of track. The Bobcat testing programme was the most comprehensive ever undertaken by Ford, and a team of seventy-five test drivers working around the clock were involved. The vehicles were often wired to a host car – usually a Ford Taunus 17M – via an umbilical cable and a mast on each vehicle to ensure the connection didn't get snagged; the host car logged all manner of parameters: speed, noise, vibration, engine and transmission temperatures, suspension loads, vertical and lateral acceleration, and so on. The remote logging avoided any unwanted effects from the half ton of recording kit – nowadays the system would be smaller and lighter.

The second Bobcat prototype totalled 200,000 miles at Lommel, and at one stage covered 45,000 miles in 120 days. From the high-speed banked circuit, the suspension-challenging cobbled Pavé and washboard, to the dust ingress shed, the water splash and rain-simulating tunnels, the design was subjected to everything. Aerodynamic testing was carried out using a one-fifth scale model in the wind tunnel at Aachen University with wet paint being used to trace the flow of air over (and under) the body; in March 1975, the tests were repeated using a full-size Bobcat at the Pininfarina design studios in Turin. By the following month, Prototype Number One – that driven by HFII and Iacocca – had been (intentionally) written off in steering column intrusion testing at Merkenich where it was drawn into a concrete wall by a winch to a precise (and repeatable) speed. Non-destructive testing for items such as seat-belt mountings was carried out on the high-speed sledge at Dunton.

The Ford test facility at Lommel in Belgium provided the venue for much of the testing. Here the suspension and body fittings get a pummelling over the cobbles – commonly referred to as Belgian Pavé. (Ford)

With the plan to sell the Bobcat all over the world, testing also had to be carried out in all types of climates; environmental test chambers are useful for initial trials, but nothing beats an in-situ test. In mid-1975, two prototypes were sent to Morocco, where they were driven mercilessly in the searing heat for several weeks with cooling and cabin ventilation being top of the list. The following winter, another couple of Bobcats were dispatched to the Arctic Circle, where they were cold-soaked for several days before cold-start testing, or simply used to check the car's performance in sub-zero conditions, with a particular focus on interior heating and window demisting.

Ford also considered the in-service cost of the Bobcat to the customer. The ever-increasing labour costs in the 1970s meant that Ford were keen to market the new car as easy and affordable not only to run, but also maintain, so maximum reliability and minimum servicing requirements were designed-in. Apart from making items such as bulb, fuse and wiper replacement easier for the owner, Ford service engineers calculated they had achieved a 20 per cent saving in routine dealer maintenance time over the company's previous best, the Escort.

Modifications Made During Testing

The wind tunnel tests led to the modification of the rear of the roof. The early design suffered excessive turbulence and drag as the air flow broke away halfway along the panel. Adding a small, aerodynamic spoiler in the form of the now trademark upward trailing edge of no more than the thickness of a pencil improved road holding and fuel consumption. The tests also verified that the late addition of the grille with its aerofoil section slats was also of benefit; at low speeds air passed into the radiator unimpeded, but at higher speeds a boundary layer formed on each slat, diverting most of the air over the bonnet, reducing drag and helping vehicle stability. Similar designs of the (Ford patented) grille found their way onto every model, even the Transit van. Another feature added after testing was the deeper front air dam which controlled the air flow under the car and reduced the susceptibility to crosswinds. The front was made as smooth as possible with minimal gaps around the headlamps, and wind noise was kept in check by making the side windows flush, improving the windscreen seal and stopping the gutter at the top of the front pillars. Many tests were carried out in the wind tunnel and dozens of minor adjustments were made to the body, but it is the roofline, air dam and grille which are the easiest to spot and added form to function. The shape of Bobcat worked too; the car had a drag coefficient of just over 0.4 – the best of any Ford at that time.

The mechanical design of the prototypes was satisfactory bar a few modifications here and there to gearchange linkage and steering geometry, but the testing programme did reveal a problem in the rear suspension. The MacPherson strut system at the front – instead of the originally considered double torsion bar arrangement – was fine and, with its use on many other models over a couple of decades, Ford were very used to it. The independent set-up at the rear, however, was too soft and the tail drifted sideways under heavy cornering. The solution – albeit a drastic one – was to completely redesign it; a coil-sprung beam axle located by two longitudinal radius arms and a Panhard rod for lateral rigidity was selected. It was no longer independent, but it worked much better and

Lommel also had a water trough. This kind of test ensures the lack of body leaks, and explores the effects of a thorough engine and underside drenching. It also helps determine if windscreen wiper performance is acceptable. (Ford)

was deemed acceptable, although there were questions initially surrounding its robustness. To silence those doubters, the test drivers deliberately spun the prototype vehicles around a dozen times sideways into a kerb before the Panhard rod could be made to buckle and even then, the car could still be driven, and the body mountings were undamaged.

To demonstrate the level of detail that was considered during the development of the new car, even the headlights received special attention. During the early 1970s, most car manufacturers started to move away from the traditional, sealed beam circular headlamps and adopted rectangular, sometimes larger, items that better blended into the design of the car. These new units were more expensive and, to keep maintenance costs down, a move was taken to revert to interchangeable bulbs popular before sealed beam units came on the scene in the early 1960s, but there was a problem. The heat generated by the bulbs warmed the air inside which expanded and escaped. As the unit cooled, it sucked in the damp air from outside causing moisture to accumulate and fog the glass. Most manufacturers tried – unsuccessfully – to seal the units and their bulbs with rubber gaskets, but the Ford engineers took a more imaginative approach. It was decided that management was better than resistance, and they provided carefully positioned holes allowing the free passage of air in and out of the unit, with a drain path for any accumulated moisture; the aperture location was also carefully chosen so that water splash from rain-soaked roads could not find its way into the lamp. Another item that was the focus of engineering for reliability was the wiring loom and fuse box. Electrical connections – in cars and anywhere else for that matter – are prone to trouble resulting from vibration and corrosion, but engineers at Ford elected to make the loom and fuse box a single sub-assembly. With the connectors permanently fixed to the appropriate slots on the fuse panel, they simply could not suffer such issues and this method has since been almost universally adopted.

The importance of cost control at Ford has already been highlighted and part of the development of a vehicle includes not just the aesthetic, functional, safety and performance aspects but the cost, and therefore the profit margin, of the final product. Ford continues to this day to keep close tabs on cost – always quoted in dollars inside the Ford empire – at all stages of the life cycle of all models and the Bobcat was no exception. Careful selection of components as well as the choice of production methods can shave a few cents off here and there. The decision to not use a nave plate or hubcap on the road wheels saved a couple of dollars, and fifty cents or so of spend was avoided by reusing the passenger grab handle from the Escort as the interior door handles on the lower specification Bobcats. The new engine and transmission, despite being a more complicated front-wheel-drive design, had fewer parts than the more conventional set-up from the Escort and so saved a bit more. Reducing the materials in a car benefits the owner too with a reduction in weight providing a corresponding improvement in fuel economy: the panel seams were trimmed on the non-structural side of spot welds; internal panels were relieved (reduced in bulk or area) in specific areas such as behind side and door trims with a bonus that repair would be simpler; holes were cut in the rear suspension radius arms; and so the relentless cost and weight savings went on. Nothing to compromise the safety or performance of the Bobcat, of course; it was just the bottom line that was being addressed as well as the headline fuel consumption figures. As an aside, the Bobcat would be the first Ford to feature bonded-on badges; the holes used to fix the Ford logo and model insignia had long since been a source of corrosion and unsightliness. The fact that it was quicker to apply stuck-on emblems and therefore less costly to build, was not mentioned in the brochure...

Now that project Bobcat was designed and developed, it had to be built in enough numbers to satisfy the predicted sales level.

5

Building the Bobcat

Developing a new car is a series of many parallel processes and, while the stylists and engineers were at work and the marketing teams were gathering their results from focus groups, production engineers were considering not only where to build the car but *how* to build it. For Ford, there was a lot at stake with the Bobcat: it was a new class of car, it was aimed at various markets around the world and, relatively late in development, a decision had been made to adopt front-wheel drive – an almost unknown area for the American company. With production planned to start in the summer of 1976, work on the plant and factories began nearly five years before and it wasn't as simple as just finding adequate capacity in an existing Ford factory and building the new car; there were many other factors at stake. Research had shown that the Bobcat wouldn't steal many existing sales, but the predicted ones would be an *addition*. Very good news but, depending upon the numbers involved, this would entail at least a major extension to an existing plant and possibly the construction of a new one. Ford had always planned that the new small car would initially be built across two or three sites in Europe, with Saarlouis in Germany being one and a completely new plant being another, but with the option of Dagenham topping up production if necessary and possibly, in time, additional locations much further afield. On the western edge of Germany, the factory at Saarlouis had opened in 1970, and started producing first the Escort and, from the following year, the Capri.

Spain

In the late 1960s, HFII and Lee Iacocca knew that the Spanish market was one of the principal areas for expansion. Unfortunately, importing anything into Spain at that time was very difficult; the dictator Francisco Franco had risen to power during the Spanish Civil War and, following the defeat of the Spanish Republic in 1939, he enforced a mercantilism regime to maximise exports but minimise imports – the country was basically closed to foreign goods. In the early 1970s, Spanish-built items had to incorporate at least 95 per cent 'domestic content', any imported components were subjected to a 30 per cent tariff and foreign companies were not allowed to hold more than a 49 per cent stake in a

Spanish-based manufacturer. Franco died in November 1975 and was succeeded by Juan Carlos I who was expected to continue with Franco's legacy; instead, however, Juan Carlos introduced reforms to dismantle the Francoist regime and to begin the Spanish transition to democracy. Fortunately for Ford, that there would be a change had become apparent as early as 1970, when the company approached Spanish government officials about setting up a business in Spain and the response was positive – or certainly not negative. The forecasts showed that in 1976, Ford would need an additional capacity of 140,000 to cope with the increase in demand for existing models, but this would not be enough to justify building a new factory. With the inclusion of the predicted sales of around 100,000 small cars in Spain, however, a new plant *would* become a necessity, and to help circumvent some of the import restrictions but take advantage of the indigenous market, Spain would be an ideal location. Even before his appointment as head of state, the car enthusiast Juan Carlos had become a passionate advocate for the Bobcat project and provided much-needed support to Ford for production to start in his country.

Spain might seem an unusual choice for a brand-new factory with untried workers and infrastructure, and the country still reeling from several decades of dictatorship. For Ford, however, it made perfect sense. Apart from the unequivocal market potential and the research which showed that the country needed a small and affordable car, Spain had a glut of workers and managing the finances of the Bobcat would help recoup the development costs in just a few years. Once the decision for a new factory had been made, HFII and his team started serious negotiations with the Spanish government both in Detroit and locally in Madrid, and they managed to secure a less restrictive business practice in return for the potential investment benefit to Spain. Ford were still required to export at least 66 per cent of the plant's production – although that fitted in with its plans anyway – and restrict its penetration of the Spanish market to less than 10 per cent.

Valencia

On 14 June 1973, following several months of discussions with the Spanish and considerations over the location for the new factory – including many thousands of letters direct from the inhabitants of various locations asking 'Señor Ford' to build the new factory near them – a decision was made. A 270-acre site north of the town of Almussafes, in the province of Valencia, was purchased. With a population of around 750,000 and the Río Turia leading to the Mediterranean Sea just a few kilometres away to the east, Valencia had a pool of willing workers and was well-placed for transport links. Ford España, the Spanish subsidiary of Ford of Europe, was created just three months after site selection on 26 September, with Carl Levy as chairman.

Work on the Valencia site began when the bulldozers moved in on 19 January 1974. One of Ford's tasks was to smooth the views of the current occupants – many of them farmers with smallholdings – and establish a fair price to buy their land. With help from the local mayor, eventually all 600 or so gave up their plots with less than a dozen disgruntled landowners needing a little additional financial persuasion. The land acquired by Ford had been orange groves and fields of onions and artichokes, all of which had previously done well in both foreign and domestic markets. With fierce and growing competition from producers in North Africa and Israel, however, most of the farmers were somewhat less than upset that reliable (and very well-paid) factory work would soon be available *and* the high-volume and profitable exports would benefit the long-term Spanish economy too. Hanns Brand, who had been responsible for the Saarlouis plant in his home country of Germany, was appointed director of operations at Valencia and his previous success shone through.

The first pre-production engine came off the Spanish assembly line on 22 September 1975, with the production units starting on 1 March the following year. On 15 December 1975, Bobcat was formally changed from a development project to a production one and, barring any major and must-fix problems that might have been reported from the still-progressing endurance testing programmes, the entire design was then frozen. To allow the assembly process to settle down, it was a Ford policy of the time that no other changes would be introduced until at least ninety days after production started; the company was well used to changes being introduced after that and pragmatically viewed them – no matter how trivial – simply as a process of continued product improvement. Given that the concrete in the factory in Valencia must have been barely set and with many inexperienced workers building a brand-new car and needing a period of training, it is perhaps not surprising that it would be the German plant that would build the first production Bobcat, and it emerged from Saarlouis on 10 May 1976. It was these cars, with their engines from Valencia, that formed the launch party for journalists and the public alike. On 18 October that year, one month ahead of the schedule imposed by HFII two years previously but after the launch on the Continent, the first Bobcat emerged from Valencia. This success boded very well for a new site designed to build 1,000 cars each day and 420,000 engines each year. As planned, and to further bolster numbers to address the incredible demand for the new car, Dagenham became operational in early 1977, although this had been delayed by the necessity of transferring the production of the Granada from Britain to Cologne. The German plant had already built Ford's flagship model and could accommodate an extra 100 cars per day, and Dagenham needed the space for a daily total of 400 Fiestas. For similar reasons, Saarlouis had moved most of its Escort production to Halewood, the Merseyside plant opened in 1963 to ease pressure on Dagenham. Once the three sites were up and running, each factory built both left-hand and right-hand drive versions to suit any market.

When the Valencia site ran at full capacity, over 9,000 workers would be required to build engines and bodywork, as well as to work on the final assembly of the Bobcat. Following labour agreements between Ford and the Spanish government, training for the workers was shared fifty-fifty, with eighty selected Spanish specialists being flown to the Ford site at Cologne in Germany or Dagenham in Britain for various technical training courses. There was never a concern about a lack of Spaniards being keen to work at Valencia, with hundreds of applications received before the site was even close to opening, and without Ford needing to advertise. With reports of relatively generous pay, Ford also received applications from workers at the SEAT factory in Barcelona (SEAT, or Sociedad Española de Automóviles de Turismo, is a Spanish car manufacturer now part of the Volkswagen Group). Ford was very aware of international relations, providing fully funded language courses in Spanish and English; they also paid a Dutch relationship expert to train the American managers and supervisors on how to behave towards the Spanish staff. Such was

In 1976, the first Ford Fiesta rolled off the new production line at Valencia in Spain. This is a fairly recent aerial shot and, with a capacity of 450,000 vehicles a year and 8,000 employees, it is one of Ford's largest manufacturing complexes outside the US. (Ford)

the efficacy of the work by Ford to integrate the Valencian population into the organisation, within six years of the factory opening most, if not all, posts were filled by locals.

Logistics

At the time of the launch of the new small Ford, the manufacturing and distribution operation was considered by many to be the most complex in the history of the industry. The whole operation had been deliberately spread around the network of Ford plants across Europe, focusing as necessary on each location's individual specialism and local requirements; this move also avoided relying on one site for the new car which was expected to be one of Ford's most important European – if not global – products since the Model T. With the Valencia, Saarlouis and Dagenham sites all planned to produce the Bobcat, the aim was that (apart from the information revealed by the Vehicle Identification Number) a British-built car would be indistinguishable from one made in Germany, and they in turn would be identical to the Spanish product. Assembling the selfsame cars from a similar mix of sub-assemblies and individual components, some of which were produced at any one of the European plants, meant this three-way production puzzle required a complex logistical setup to service it.

All the engines for the new Ford were built at Valencia using cylinder heads, blocks and crankshafts cast using the blast furnaces at Dagenham, although, if necessary, the British plant could also machine and assemble these components. In time, the Spanish plant expanded its capabilities and within a couple of years Valencia was able to supply around half of the castings. In line with the Ford tradition of using a toponym to name a power unit, the engine for the Bobcat was called the 'Valencia'. Carburettors were supplied by the Ford site at Belfast in Northern Ireland, and the transmissions came from the brand-new plant at Bordeaux in France but using gears and aluminium cases from Cologne. Despite a promise made by HFII to President of France Georges Pompidou that Ford would build its next car plant in France, the new site at Blanquefort near Bordeaux was focused solely on transmissions, although by the 1980s it had become the largest in Europe. The body panels were pressed in Valencia and Cologne, radiators came from Basildon in Essex and petrol tanks were made in Saarlouis. The distribution network comprised ships, rail containers and trucks carefully choreographed to ensure the correct parts arrived at the right site, and completed cars were available throughout Europe and eventually many other countries. Components from outside suppliers were collected into loads at the Ford parts consolidation centre in Daventry, in the British Midlands, before joining the other items on their way to either Spain, Saarlouis or Dagenham. Rail movement to and from Spain was limited in the earlier years of production because the track gauge was non-standard and necessitated a time-consuming axle change at the border; only since 1992 have the high-speed links on the Iberian Peninsula adopted the near international standard of 4 feet 8½ inches (1,435 mm), instead of 5 feet $5^{21}/_{32}$ inches (1,668 mm).

The logistics necessary to allow the complex supply of parts from all over Europe to operate efficiently and seamlessly was only thanks to an excellent communications network. In line with the other major car-producing plants within the Ford organisation, Valencia had a large telephone switchboard – one of the largest in Spain – and an extensive network of computers. At 9 o'clock each morning, a complete status of the availability of each of the 1,600 or so components and sub-assemblies needed to feed the ever-hungry production lines at each of the three assembly sites was assessed and delivery schedules adjusted accordingly. This 'just-in-time' (JIT) management philosophy was developed and perfected by industrial engineer Taiichi Ohno at Toyota, and sets out to avoid either a lack of or an excess of stock; it is now almost universally accepted but its use outside Japan in the 1970s was revolutionary.

Let's Call it Fiesta!

The name of a new product can be key to its success or otherwise. In the spring of 1974, the new Class B Ford remained anonymous. Those working on the project had become accustomed to the codename of Bobcat and saw no real need to change it. In the meantime, however, Mercury – a Ford brand created in 1938 – had launched their own Bobcat, so another name had to be found. Ford's marketing team kicked off an internal quest for suggestions; it needed to be short, easy to pronounce, one that went well with Ford, was inoffensive and, preferably, one with a Continental flavour; it also had to be unused by anyone else.

Like its wild cat namesake, the 1974 Mercury Bobcat is native to North America. The Mercury, however, was actually a rebadged Ford Pinto, the latter being the firm's response to the influx of smaller cars from Japan. Mercury was more upmarket than its parent Ford, and was an attempt to coax more affluent buyers into smaller vehicles. This model meant another name had to be found for Project Bobcat. (Ford)

Names flooded in, and the list of nearly 100 was whittled down to thirteen: Amigo, Bambi, Bebe, Bolero, Bravo, Cherie, Tempo, Chico, Fiesta, Forito, Metro, Pony and Sierra. After many months of deliberations, the marketing team chose four, added a latecomer, and ranked the five in order of popularity: Bravo, Fiesta, Amigo, Strada and Pony. The shortlist was then sent to Ford's lawyers to determine if any were already registered, and whether they might be available to use on the new car.

Ultimately, the choice was narrowed down to Bravo or Fiesta: Bravo belonged to an Italian spaghetti manufacturer but could be used; Fiesta was once used by Oldsmobile, and permission would be needed from General Motors (GM). HFII usually liked to make the final selection himself and, after much pacing around his office, he thought Fiesta went well with Ford and it sounded 'happy, colourful and dynamic'; that it meant feast or party in Spanish was a happy coincidence, although that feeling probably chimed with that of the Spaniards when they found out that Ford would be building the Fiesta in Valencia. When HFII called Tom Murphy – the then chairman of GM – to ask if he could use Fiesta, he was told he could have it, it was his! So, in late September 1974, the product planning committee was told that the smallest Ford up to that time was to be called Fiesta, and all that was left to do was to launch it.

6

Billion Dollar Baby

The design and development of the Ford Fiesta was no penny-pinching exercise by Ford. When Henry Ford II signed off the Bobcat project in the early 1970s, he was approving an investment of $1 billion (equivalent to $10 billion in 2024) over just four years. It is perhaps slightly ironic that, at less than 12 feet long (3.5 m), the new car was at the time the smallest ever built by Ford and represented a new sector for the company, yet it was the most expensive project in the company's history. The level of investment not only demonstrates the significant financial backing that a large organisation has, but the importance it places on getting a product absolutely *right*. Ford now needed to prepare their dealership network, launch the car and see exactly what the press, and more importantly the buying customers, really thought of the new Ford Fiesta.

Dealing with Customers

One of the advantages of owning a car produced by a large and international company is that wherever you go – within reason – you are never far from a dealer who will know how to service and repair it. Indeed, as a driver you have already taken advantage of one of the many dealers for a certain brand when you initially purchased the vehicle of your choice. This happy situation has existed since the early days of motor car ownership and Ford had – and still has – one of the most extensive dealer networks of any manufacturer. At the time of the launch of the Fiesta, there were over 6,000 dealers spread throughout Europe with 380 of them in Britain. All of these dealers needed sales and marketing information for the new car as well as an intensive training programme for the workshop staff to teach them how to service the Fiesta correctly. Several months before the Fiesta came to Britain, 320 mechanics had already received a thorough grounding in the new car at the Ford Service Training College in Daventry. By the time the Fiesta appeared in the dealers' showrooms in Britain in early 1977, more than 2,500 mechanics and 300 service managers were fully equipped to look after it.

It's not 'clear' why this transparent Fiesta was made (fibreglass panels over the colour-coded steel structure). Some companies used see-through cars at motor shows (the Hillman Imp, for example, at Earls Court in 1963) but this one looks a little rough and ready. Another possibility is that it was a training aid for mechanics. (© British Motor Industry Heritage Trust)

Launch and Reception

Following a series of carefully orchestrated leaks from Ford to the motoring press about their new baby, the Fiesta was finally unveiled to the public on 9 September 1976. Set by Ford's marketing team as the international launch date, it was initially on sale in Germany, France and certain other countries of mainland Europe but not Britain – the British public would have to wait until early the following year. Such delays are not uncommon; they sometimes result from the special engineering alterations necessary for the minority-market, right-hand drive cars. As is usually the case, since it can be conducive to fostering an early and favourable reception, the motoring press was taken into the manufacturer's confidence and made party to the information necessary to construct fully detailed articles several weeks before the launch date. Ford also took the publicity opportunity of the 1976 Le Mans 24-hour endurance race held over the weekend of 12 and 13 June, by having drawings and other details of the Fiesta on display and offering the first French example as the top prize in a competition; neither the specific trim level of the car nor the name of the winner is documented.

With the Paris Motor Show in early October 1976 just a few weeks after the European launch and the Fiesta still hot on the motoring journalists' typewriters, Ford didn't miss the opportunity. About a third of Ford's allocated space comprised a circular stand with examples of each Fiesta model lined up around the periphery, and the top specification in the middle.

All European markets – including Britain – got a similar range of models: saloon (the base model), L, S and the luxurious Ghia. With a woman by each car to point out the key features, a male announcer ran through the specifications from the base to the Ghia; his colleagues on stage then opened the doors, bonnet and boot, and – in a manner that seems a little passé today – pointed with graceful, sweeping movements to the various significant differences of each. With the Paris and the Frankfurt motor shows alternating each year, there was no suitable event for an appropriately timed unveiling in Germany. British cinemas, however, showed adverts based on footage from France with dubbing in English, timed to coincide with the UK launch; the commercial ended with the British actor Patrick Allen adding smoothly: 'Fiesta – a spectacular combination of safety, reliability, economy, ease of servicing and low cost of maintenance'. It wasn't long before the motoring press referred to the new Ford as a 'supermini' – a sobriquet first applied to the Renault 5 half a decade earlier.

Although the styling studio Ghia had provided the genesis for the Fiesta, giving the top-of-the-line trim level a similar appellation had nothing specifically to do with the (by now wholly Ford-owned) outfit in Turin, but it had a conveniently upmarket feel to it and had already been in use for over two years on the Capri II. The Italian styling link with the accompanying ornate emblem served the company well too; Ford adopted the tag across most of the company's top-specification models right up to the 2000s.

Three variants of the Valencia engine were available from launch: a 957 cc in both low- and high-compression versions of 39 and 44 bhp (the former to accommodate lower

This carefree couple have stolen a weekend away in London, and they are doubtless very proud of their new Ford Fiesta Ghia finished in Oyster Gold. Given the likelihood of the British weather turning unpleasant, one hopes they've remembered to pack the (tilt and removable) sunshine roof panel. (Ford)

quality petrol or help with local taxation), plus the more powerful 1,117 cc developing 52 bhp. The base saloon could be had with either of the smaller engines and the L could have any of the three; the sporty S model was only available with the bigger unit, and the Ghia could be ordered with either size of the standard compression engines. Even in the S, the 1,117 cc had a standard level of tune, although it did get suspension modifications, and all bigger-engined Fiestas were fitted with a brake servo.

Ford was receptive to the slightly disgruntled journalists of publications that hadn't been able to snatch a ride in one of their colleague's Continent-based Fiestas during 1976 and arranged an event in the winter of that year, especially for the British. The venue was Monte-Carlo no less, based at the exclusive Hôtel de Paris – completed in 1864 and the star of a couple of James Bond films – where a fleet of yellow Fiestas was made available for the assembled to drive around the Alpes-Maritime. Apart from the cachet of the location which doubtless placated the scribes, it was also hoped that the winter weather on the Mediterranean coast might be better than that in Britain; it was not to be, but it did mean that the car could be tested in more UK-representative climatic conditions. *Motor Sport* magazine was present and reported that Ford of Britain's Chairman and Managing Director Terry Beckett schmoozed the audience of journalists in the famous hotel and spoke eloquently about the extensive market research that had been performed. He reported that 55 per cent of drivers would be women, and 47 per cent would go to multiple car owners, where wives and their offspring were expected to use the Fiesta primarily for the weekly shop. Such figures prompted Ford to take the unprecedented move of inviting the journalists' partners and spouses along for the ride to get their very important views on the Fiesta, encouraging the drivers to swap over regularly so they could both get a good feel for the new car.

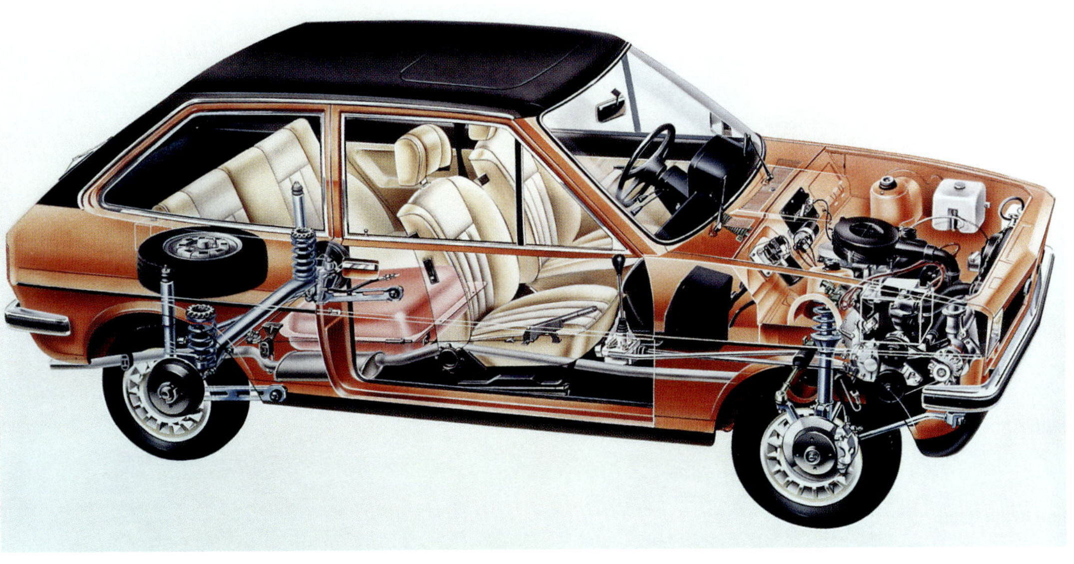

The mechanical details of the first generation Ford Fiesta are evident here: the coil-sprung rear beam axle, the Panhard rod for lateral control, the MacPherson struts at the front and the transverse engine. This graphic was used in various brochures and launch material, and allowed the press and customers to visualise the car's inner workings. (Ford)

Press Reception

The motoring press across Europe was full of information about the Ford Fiesta; it was an important car for Ford, creating a new market for their customers wanting a small car with a blue oval badge rather than a Renault, Fiat, Volkswagen or anything else. Even British readers, who would have to wait five or six months, into the new year of 1977, to see the Fiesta at their local Ford showroom, were party to extensive multi-page spreads in the various journals available – how tantalising and frustrating that must have been for some!

The British car magazine *Motor* of 17 July 1976 published an article about the new Ford Fiesta – a couple of months before it had been launched anywhere. In it, they acknowledged that Ford engineers had gone to great lengths to ensure that the car attained at least the *same* reliability and ease of repair that had been a hallmark of their mechanically simpler models. Like several other sets of journalists and scribes from all over Europe, the magazine had been given early access to the Fiesta – even being able to have a very brief drive. The article explained the salient features of the new car including the point that the Ghia had a locking compartment under the boot floor for valuables; they also reported that storage in the cabin was good with the fascia shelf, door bins and a glove-box lid for the S and Ghia. *Motor* was also complimentary about 'the three fingertip stalks' for the horn, indicators, lights and wipers. And they said the pedals 'were small but well-spaced'. The ventilation system came in for some praise – July 1976 was very hot in Europe – and the 'very effective two-speed fan was neither loud nor a damned nuisance'. Presumably the abnormally warm weather precluded a satisfactory check of the heating system.

That short test allowed the drivers to report the 'pure pleasure' of the gear change, adding that Ford had already set that standard with the Escort, and the front-wheel drive Fiesta didn't

Presumably a certain Cruella de Vil has left the scene to collect another ninety-seven of the little spotted canines... It's amazing what one can fit in the rear hatch of the Ford Fiesta – seen here with the rear seat already folded in preparation for the rest of the load. (Ford)

let that slip at all. A decent change also needs a light and progressive clutch and, apparently, the cable-operated system with its clever rachet, self-adjusting mechanism was well up to scratch, although some other reports thought it was a 'bit sharp'. *Motor* magazine also delved deeper into some of the mechanical features and spotted that, instead of the thicker (but heavier) driveshafts favoured by Fiat for the 'longer' side of the transmission, Ford fitted a torsional damper to take out some of the vibrations but stuck to similarly-sized shafts. Further details described the suspension system, explaining the rear suspension with its Panhard rod was devoid of upper radius arms but had straps welded to the damper locations thus avoiding excessive boot area intrusion. At the front, the 'straightforward' MacPherson system was slightly different from most in that a pair of rubber-bushed compression links replaced the usual U-shaped front anti-roll bar found during testing to be unnecessary. The strut mountings also featured low-friction bearings made from Polytetrafluoroethylene (PTFE or 'Teflon') to prevent the coil springs winding up, giving lighter steering at parking speeds. Several reports did suggest that the ride was a little 'jittery' at low speeds, but the car handled well and was fun to drive – 'lively' one of them said. In the March 1977 issue of *Popular Motoring,* the reporter praised the ease with which the exhaust, sump and suspension struts could be removed; the publication was, after all, aimed at the do-it-yourself mechanic. If there was any doubt about the slightly dated features of the Valencia engine when compared with its competitors, *Autocar* published an article at the time of the UK launch written by the magazine's go-to expert on such matters, Olaf Fersen. Having queried the use of just three main bearings and the lack of the then-emerging toothed-rubber, belt-driven, overhead camshaft mounted in an aluminium cylinder head, Olaf was told by Ford engineers that it passed their standard 180-hour test (just over one week) under full load and at 6,000 rpm; they added that the valve gear would be reliable up to 7,000 and, as such, it would be perfect for the high-speed autobahns where speed limits were occasionally absent.

In March 1977, *Car* magazine's 'Giant Test' of the Fiesta against its five main opponents, including the Mini, the Renault 5 and the Fiat 127, thought the (more expensive) Volkswagen Polo to be the victor, but praised the Ford for its fuel economy and reduced maintenance requirements. The magazine suggested that the husbands of the women drivers Ford had aimed the car at would love the low running costs. This *was* the 1970s remember...

What You Got for Your Money

At launch in the UK on 2 February 1977 when the Fiesta finally appeared at British dealers, it was priced from £1,856 (GBP) for a 957 cc base saloon (the low- and high-compression options were similarly priced) up to £2,756.93 for a 1,117 cc Ghia. The prices included VAT (Value Added Tax), but delivery was always quoted as a separate charge of £49, with more for Northern Ireland and the Channel Islands. It is interesting to note that the bottom of the range Escort Popular undercut the base Fiesta by £57 – but this oddity would be rectified within a couple of years. The base saloon was quite spartan and made do without a rear parcel shelf, heated rear window and halogen headlamps; it had black painted bumpers instead of chrome items and non-reclining seats with fixed belts. The L solved these deficiencies and gained bright side window trim, black painted sills, dipping rear view mirror, storage bins, more soundproofing and houndstooth pattern fabrics.

A 1981 Fiesta 1100S – the first sporting Fiesta denoted by the side stripes complete with the 'S' model designation and deckchair pattern seats. The glass sunroof and the alloy wheels were optional extras. (Ford)

For the enthusiastic buyer, the 1100S lived up to its sporting pretensions with a four-spoke steering wheel, illuminated heater controls, 'S' side and rear stripes, striped seat fabric, a rev counter and a clock (the latter in a centre console), sports suspension, intermittent wipers with an electric windscreen washer pump (on lesser models it was a foot-operated rubber pump) and a rear anti-roll bar. The Ghia got all this (apart from the stiffer springs and the stickers), but also benefited from alloy wheels, appropriate enamelled badges, a rear wash-wipe, a mahogany effect instrument binnacle, a push button MW/LW radio nestling in a similarly finished centre console and what Ford described as a 'luxury' interior. One seemingly small item, but one which received many plaudits, was the rear hatch 'twistlock' fitted only to the top specification; this meant one didn't always need the key to open the boot and must have saved many potential lock-out incidents over the coming years.

Despite any criticisms about specifications, the Fiesta was well-equipped for the time with a host of safety features that Ford was keen to point out in its brochure: dual-circuit brakes (discs on the front), two-speed wipers, hazard warning flashers, steel-braced radial ply tyres, 25 square feet of glass area (the best of any small car) with 309 degrees of visibility and a collapsible steering column. The petrol tank was also mounted ahead of the rear axle to protect it from a rear impact. Reliability and servicing costs were also more favourable than many other cars with self-adjusting clutch and brakes, maintenance-free front and rear wheel bearings, see-through fluid containers under the bonnet, single-piece exhaust fitted *under* the rear axle for easy replacement and the availability of 'part' body panels for reduced cost accident repairs plus a lower insurance rating. Economy was a big selling point too with Ford's 'sonic idle' carburettor which leaned off the idle mixture in traffic, a wind-tunnel designed body, a high-ratio top gear for more relaxed cruising and an electric cooling fan to avoid robbing the engine of any horsepower (more powerful and thermostatically controlled on the 1,117 cc engine – it 'droned incessantly' on the smaller engines, one tester complained). Customers could rectify many of the specification shortcomings by ticking the various options: a heated rear window for £35, a rear fog lamp for less than £15 or perhaps a radio for less than £70. These may sound laughably affordable now but factor in inflation and a customer might have thought twice.

One of the interior colours available from the launch of the Fiesta in 1976 included orange door cards with matching orange and black houndstooth-patterned fabric seats. Other notable colours included a fluorescent green, or Regency Green as Ford named it. Note the useful door pockets. (Author)

The Ghia had more luxurious velour finished seats. The latch, allowing the front seats to fold forward for access to the rear, can also be seen here. The black plastic block towards the top of the seat edge is the fixing for the 'assist straps' (as the brochure stated) on the back of the front seats. (Ford)

Ford was justifiably very proud of its new car; brochures and magazine adverts carried the lines: 'The New Ford Fiesta – Oh what a beautiful baby!' and 'For a baby, it's pretty big'. There was even a touch of the Churchillian with, 'Never has so much advanced engineering gone into a small car'. Despite the praise and the hyperbole there must, however, have been some consternation at senior management level within Ford that it would take several years to recoup the massive development costs of the Fiesta. But it would be worth it; the Fiesta stayed toward the top of the best-seller lists in many countries and across seven versions for nearly five decades; it is rightly recognised as a World Car.

Above: Ford were keen to advertise their new car as small, but wanted to point out that the inside still had plenty of room (for a family and a kite at least) even in this basic model. (Ford)

Left: Another one of Ford's marketing lines. Ford were justifiably proud of its new, 'beautiful' offspring – in this case an S version with the standard striped seats but optional head restraints and alloy wheels. (Ford)

7

The Classic Fiestas

To describe the seven basic versions of the Ford Fiesta, this book has elected to categorise the cars into two broad sections: Classic and Twenty-First Century. Apologies are due to those owners who may (understandably) consider their post-1999 Fiesta to be a classic, but it serves as a convenient split. Within these two groups (and putting aside the sporty and other derivatives for the time being), a 'generation' number is used: one to seven. The term 'mark' is not used since there has been some confusion over the total number; some publications report seven, which matches the generations, but others – due to a facelift being erroneously counted as a new mark – quote eight.

First Generation (1976–83)

It wouldn't be very long before the Ford Fiesta proved itself to be very successful. Within the first year alone half a million were built – it was Europe's fastest-selling car with one in four Fords sold being a Fiesta – and in 1981, with 7.5 per cent of the market, the little Ford was Britain's third best-seller behind two of its stablemates: the Cortina and the Escort. The Fiesta was unstoppable!

Daz Newall's 1981 957cc first generation Popular Plus in Dove Grey. The nicely contrasting side stripe, which complements the brown interior, was probably a dealer fitment. The rear fog light was, incidentally, a legal requirement in the UK from 1 October 1979. (Author)

The Fiesta received formal praise too. The Design Council makes several awards each year but only one or two are appropriate to the motor car, and the new car had already benefited from two: it used a derivative of Ford's R-module instrument cluster from the facelifted Mk3 Cortina which had won in 1974 and, as already noted, it was fitted with the sonic idle carburettor, another winner for the company from the following year. In 1978, however, Ford received a third award but this time for the Fiesta as a whole. It was the first time in the history of the Design Council that a complete car had won; the judges considered that the Fiesta was the first to have been designed with reduced cost and ease of maintenance in mind right from the start, and 'set the pace amongst competitive manufacturers both in the UK and abroad'. The Fiesta was also expected to win the 1977 European Car of the Year award (ECotY), but ended up in third place behind the winning Rover SD1 and second-place Audi 100. The small Ford never did win the coveted ECotY but came third for a second time in 1990.

In September 1977, the Fiesta range was expanded with the addition of a 1.3-litre engine; it was initially only for the S and Ghia, but it was later available on all models from the L upwards. Not simply an enlarged version of the Valencia units, the new 1,298 cc motor with its twin-choke carburettor was a derivative of the trusted five main-bearing Kent engine from the Escort and Cortina, and gave a useful power advantage of 13 bhp over the 1,117 cc item.

Even in the Popular Plus, the interior was a nice place to be. It has fabric seats and even has a centre console with a clock but no radio. Note the foot-operated, rubber-plunger windscreen washer pump just in view behind the console – on the S and Ghia models it was electric and finger-tip operated. (Author)

At the start of the 1970s, several car manufacturers started to produce limited editions – sometimes referred to as 'special' editions – of certain models, and Ford was no exception. A cynic might suggest that they provide a means by which old versions are used up in an enticingly packaged and priced product, and indeed these 'run-out' (or 'sell-down' in Ford parlance) models are sometimes available towards the end of production; another reason might be that it's a fillip to boost flagging sales, or to promote a product which may have fallen into a shadow following the launch of a competitor's new car; manufacturers also create limited editions to highlight a specific event or point in the company's history. Whatever the reason, these models benefit the customer with various options usually at very little (or no) cost over the base product, and fall into two broad types: dealer created or factory produced. The latter tend to be more favourably viewed by the used car market since they are seen as an official product, with some having since become rare and priced accordingly.

The 957 cc 'Valencia' engine in Daz's 1981 Popular Plus. Note the thermostatic electric fan, the translucent bottles for ease of checking the coolant and washer fluid, plus the accessibility of the service items such as the battery, coil and the air cleaner. The alloy bell-housing and transmission are evident too. (Author)

The Fiesta has a similar folding seat and hinged lid arrangement as the Fiat 127 and the Renault 5. The boot floor has been removed in this shot giving access to the spare wheel and tools. On the Ghia, the right-hand portion had a lockable lid to secure the valuables that most other Fiesta drivers presumably didn't own. (Author)

Over sixty Fiesta-based limited editions were created – too many to list here – and one of the first was the Solitaire in June 1978. Based on the 1100L, it was available in either black or white, with blue or tan trim based on that in the Ghia. With only 2,000 built, the Solitaire celebrated the seventy-fifth anniversary of the creation by Henry Ford of the Ford Motor Company in Dearborn. In February 1979 after just twenty-nine months of production, the Ford Fiesta hit a milestone of its own with the 1 millionth car to roll off the production line – the fastest European Ford to reach the total. To celebrate this landmark, Ford released a limited edition version based on the Fiesta L model and named it the Fiesta Million. Just over 3,000 Fiesta Millions were produced, all in either black or silver and fitted with a host of special features: black bumpers with red inserts, red side stripes, black window surrounds, a reversing light, tinted glass, check seats, head restraints, a centre console with a clock and a radio cassette, and a heated rear window. Yet another special model was produced in June 1981. Finished in either grey or blue metallic over silver, and with a choice of 1.1 or 1.3 engines, the Bravo was built to celebrate the 2 millionth Fiesta; based on the L model, it was fitted with a sunroof and a centre console.

With the oil prices higher than ever in North America and to provide US and Canadian Ford buyers with a solution, the first-generation Fiesta was also produced in 1.6-litre 'Federal' specification, again using the Kent engine as the basis. According to the brochure for the 'Front Wheel Drive Fiesta', the car was 'Built in Germany', and embodied 'a scientific combination of features that result in driver benefits which are surprising for cars in its price class'. It then described some of those features including the Weber carburettor – 'the brand used in Ferrari' it reminded the reader, along with the 'smooth, spirited action' of the four-speed floor

In October 1978, the limited edition 'Kingfisher' was announced. A thousand were finished in two-tone metallic blue and silver, but single-tone – 750 of each – was also available at a saving of £200. Based on the 1100L, it had a few Ghia luxuries: radio, sunroof, rim embellishers, upgraded seats and a clock. In Ford's words, 'As eye-catching as it is exclusive'. (Ford)

shift transmission. Federal Fiestas were (as the sales literature promised) built in Germany rather than either Britain or Spain since, to the American market, cars of German origin were perceived to be of high quality. Differences for the US included 5 mph impact-safe bumpers, circular headlamps (anything else contravened regulations) and amber side marker lamps. Among the options not available in Europe was air conditioning which, along with the California-friendly but power-sapping emissions and smog control equipment, meant the bigger engine was very necessary. In the autumn of 1980, and after selling a respectable 263,000 units, the US market for the Fiesta dried up; the pressure on fuel costs had eased and the company had already announced the arrival of the bigger Escort. At the end of 1979, and with the success of the Ford Escort (over 6 million were built at Saarlouis between 1970 and 1988, the plant's main product), German production of the Fiesta was moved to Cologne.

In February 1980 meanwhile, the European range was expanded with the inclusion of a GL model to bridge the gap between the L and the Ghia. With halogen headlamps, better seat fabric, a console with clock and radio, a brake servo and a choice of 1.1 or 1.3 engines, the new model was well equipped. At the start of the following year, another pair were added to the

For a French feel to your photograph, include a Citroën 2CV; for a German one, you need a ski hut, a lederhosen-clad Bavarian and a sign written in the Fraktur typeface. In the 1970s, US buyers wanted economy but with German quality, and the Fiesta was a good option. Note the low-speed, impact-resistant bumpers, side-marker lamps and the circular headlights. (Ford)

Fiesta family in the form of the bottom of the range Popular and the slightly better equipped Popular Plus. These specific additions finally removed the price anomaly between the original base Fiesta and the lower-priced, yet larger, Escort Popular. The name 'Popular' had been resurrected from the budget models of old, including the 1932 Model Y, the first metal-bodied £100 saloon and the first UK-specific Ford produced at Dagenham. With non-reclining vinyl seats, a rubber floor covering, no heated rear window or rear wiper, the Fiesta Popular was very basic and aimed at fleet buyers; the additions with the Plus included fabric seats, carpet, two sun visors, the option of the bigger engine and, being very keenly priced, it sold well.

There was a final flurry for the first-generation Fiesta in 1982 when a set of general improvements were made: wider, wrap-around black bumpers, illuminated switches across all specifications, better seats, more compliant suspension, a rear parcel tray on the L (with carpet inserts on the GL) and electronic ignition for the 1300. In April of that year, there was an option of an economy version of the 1,117 cc engine (as well as both versions of the smaller unit); this tune of engine resulted in slightly *more* power and torque, along with an improvement of 5 mpg over the standard 1.1, thus achieving its aim.

The special edition 'Firefly', announced in June 1980, was available in Strato Silver, Cordoba Beige, Signal Red or – like the one seen here – Terracotta. With a choice of 957 or 1,117 cc engines, a three-colour side decal plus the seats and suspension from the S, the fully colour-coded Firefly was described by Ford as, 'A Bright New Style Setter'. (Ford)

Above: Most manufacturers were looking at saving fuel – it was a major selling point after all – and Ford was no exception. The Fuel Economy Research Vehicle (FERV) was based on a first generation Fiesta. Seen here on test, it had a smoother front end and a rear spoiler which saved 10 per cent drag and, with its higher gearing, meant that over 70 mpg was possible. (Burgess-Wise)

Below: Conveniently showing the minor tweaks (different bumpers, for example) of the facelifted first generation, the limited edition Quartz appeared in January 1983, and 'Timed to Perfection', the brochure stated. Based on the Popular Plus, the full palette of colours was available and it came with red wheel rings and wide, side decals. (Ford)

Second Generation (1983–89)

The second generation of the Fiesta unveiled in 1983 appeared to be little more than a facelift of the first resulting in a softer shape with better aerodynamics, the most obvious difference being the 'drooped' nose. Sales of the Austin Metro, launched a couple of years before, had surpassed the Fiesta during 1982 and 1983, and the motoring press expressed some doubts about whether the minor updates would redress the balance.

Although the new car looked like its predecessor, many changes were under the skin. The 957 and 1,117 cc Valencia overhead valve (OHV) engines continued but with minor improvements to power, torque and economy. The entire front end from the door hinge forward was new and, apart from the styling changes, inner wing modifications and a higher bonnet line allowed the updated (and physically larger) engines to be

The second generation Fiesta. Note the curves, the less pronounced grille and the bigger (13 instead of 12 inch) wheels. Apart from aerodynamic improvements, the front panelwork changes allowed various physically bigger engines to be fitted, including the diesel unit from the Escort. The mudflaps on Paul Biggs' February 1985 1.1 Popular Plus are an aftermarket fitment. (Author)

Little has really changed with the rear of the second generation other than rounding-off, in keeping with design trends of the time. The two reversing lights (previously a mid-mounted single on the valance) are now incorporated in the rear lamp clusters, although the rear fog light is still a bit of an afterthought. (Author)

The interior of the second generation Fiesta acquired an instrument binnacle based upon that in the Sierra, and a more modern look to the seats. The elegantly simple yet ergonomic layout of the switchgear is evident here. A fire extinguisher in any car, let alone a forty-year-old car, is a sensible accessory. (Author)

The 1,117 cc engine in this second generation Fiesta is a familiar sight. One or two ancillaries have been moved around and all models now have a brake servo along with a thermostatic air intake (improving warm-up performance). The battery cut-out device is a relatively recent aftermarket addition. (Author)

accommodated. New to the Fiesta was the 1.3-litre overhead camshaft (OHC) petrol unit first used in the 1980 Mk3 Escort and it replaced the Kent engine of similar displacement. Also introduced was an all-new Dagenham-built 53 bhp 1,608 cc OHC normally aspirated (i.e. non-turbocharged) diesel – the first production engine with a plastic inlet manifold. A further boost to the Fiesta's economy was a five-speed gearbox. It wasn't available on the smallest petrol unit; it was optional on the 1100, but standard on the 1.3 and the diesel. The latter proved quite a hit with driving schools too, being frugal and harder to stall.

The OHC petrol engine is worthy of a mention. A hemispherical cylinder head ('hemi') is one of the best shapes for a combustion chamber. With an inlet and exhaust valve pointing outwards from each side of the dome-shaped head, it provides an efficient flow of gases across the chamber. The hemi can be implemented using two rocker shafts but Ford were keen to move to an OHC layout. The double overhead camshaft (DOHC) design is the classic and elegant method but it was costly to build, so Ford engineers compromised.

The outward-pointing valves, with an included angle of 45 degrees, were each operated by a rocker from a belt-driven, single camshaft running centrally in an aluminium head on a cast-iron block. To cater for each cylinder's inlet-exhaust cam lobe separation but ensuring gas flow was as near as possible across the head, each rocker was twisted 7 degrees in plan. Named the 'Compound Valve-angle Hemispherical' (CVH) engine after its three-dimensional puzzle of angles, in 68 bhp 1,296 cc form it gave both the Escort and the Fiesta a worthwhile boost in power and mechanical refinement over the OHV units.

Left: A slice through the Compound Valve-angle Hemispherical (CVH) cylinder head. It shows the camshaft in the middle of the aluminium head, and the two valves per cylinder operated from the inclined and twisted rockers. Together they form a close-to-ideal crossflow path for the gasses in the near-hemispherical head. (Unknown source)

Below: The CVH engine in one of its natural habitats! This is a January 1989 second generation XR2 with the 96 bhp 1,597 cc unit from the Escort XR3. With its five-speed gearbox, it's a snug fit but it made for a fun package, and it remains sought after today. Buyers would have to wait for the third generation of Fiesta before they could enjoy petrol injection. (Author)

Inside, the dashboard was totally different, and the seats and general trim had been improved. With Popular, Popular Plus, L and Ghia variants available as well as a sporty version in the pipeline, the updates were useful, but the motoring press lamented the absence of a five-door version for which they would have to wait another six years. In 1986, there was a push to make vehicles cleaner, and the emissions of carbon monoxide (CO) and nitrogen oxides (NOx) were the targets. For the CVH unit, Ford elected to make the engine work satisfactorily with a much leaner mixture of petrol and air by modifying the combustion chamber shape to ensure more complete combustion. The resulting 1.4-litre 'lean burn' engine (1,392 cc) was more powerful (74 bhp), and economy rose by nearly 10 per cent. Despite the success, the legislators mandated the 'catalytic converter', and lean burn was short-lived.

In 1987, the first automatic Fiesta appeared with a Continuously Variable Transmission (Ford called it CTX), developed as a joint project with Fiat and using patents from DAF, a Dutch company which had developed their similar 'Variomatic' system several decades earlier. With steel segmented belts instead of the usual rubber and textile, clutchless driving was a

Based on the third generation Fiesta, the 'Urba' was Ford's concept of the ideal city car. With automatic parking aids, a built-in garage door opener, a fridge in the boot for the shopping, loads of storage and two doors on the nearside but just the driver's on the offside into the traffic, the designers seem to have thought of everything. (Ford)

The Tuareg concept was a joint project between the Dearborn and Ghia design studios. As a mini-SUV, it may have only been 1,117 cc but it had raised suspension, split tailgate, extra lights, Wolfrace polished alloy wheels and bold decals. Unveiled at the 1979 Geneva Motor Show, Ford said it was 'a practical, off-road, desert Fiesta'. (Burgess-Wise)

welcome outcome but in practice it proved awkward for the driver; discussions at a senior level presumably took place when a consumer programme on British television demonstrated a CTX-equipped Fiesta (a system also on the Fiat Uno) struggling to reverse up quite a gentle slope.

Ford continued to take advantage of its limited editions for the second-generation Fiesta. In June 1986 – the seventy-fifth anniversary of Ford manufacturing in Britain – the very timely Holiday appeared based on a five-speed 1.1-litre Popular Plus with side stripes and a suitable sticker on the tailgate. The following summer, the Bonus provided a budget Fiesta which undercut the cheapest model by around £400 and was available in either silver or black with white wheel covers.

Welcome to the Bebop! Another Ghia design exercise, this was an attempt to jazz up the existing Fiesta pickups (the Bantam and the Courier) which had sold all over the world (but not in the UK). With extra lights, a few bits nicked from the RS parts store and stiffening bars for the pickup bed, this one went nowhere. (Ford)

In 1978, Ford made an attempt at a 'transformable' vehicle; that is, one car that could do everything, and this is it. The Fiesta Fantasy was a pickup (depicted here) with a set of add-on parts to become a 2+2 coupé, an estate or an open-top roadster. The assumption was one had the space to store all the bits of transforming plastic... (Ford)

Third Generation (1989–97)

By the late 1980s and with annual sales lingering in third or fourth place, the Fiesta was long overdue a complete revamp. Despite the facelift in 1983 and overall sales of 5 million, it now lagged dramatically behind the competition in almost every department: passenger accommodation, the lack of a five-door version, luggage space, performance and driving involvement. After five years and an investment of more than £550 million, the new Fiesta was launched in February 1989. It boasted a stiffer, stronger, wider bodyshell better protected against corrosion, with an increased wheelbase promising to fix all the highlighted shortcomings (indeed, it was now best in class for interior space). Everything about the new car was different; very little had been carried across and it could finally compete with the Fiat Uno and Peugeot 205 as a more 'grown-up' supermini.

Codenamed BE13, the third-generation Fiesta was a dramatic improvement over its predecessor and finally offered both three- and five-door versions. The two smaller Valencia OHV engines were carried over but enlarged slightly to 999 and 1,118 cc with redesigned cylinder heads to slightly raise power and torque, but reduce emissions and fuel consumption. The modified units were marketed as 'High Compression Swirl' (HCS). Research had shown that most Fiesta journeys were much less than 10 miles long by which time the engine had barely warmed up which, apart from the occupants being cold and the windows not being fully demisted, meant the engine had not reached its most efficient temperature for reduced fuel economy *and* emissions. Ford's engineers reduced the volume of coolant in the engine's cylinder head and specified a more progressive thermostat with the result that, coupled with the electric fan, the engine warmed up quickly in the winter but didn't overheat in the summer. To improve reliability, the HCS units acquired

The third generation of the Ford Fiesta was completely new. This is a 1990 three-door L with a fuel-injected 1.1-litre OHV petrol engine with a catalytic converter. Note the bright bumper inserts and the full wheel covers. The driver might well be enjoying some music from their Ford 'Premium Sound 2000' radio. (Ford)

a crank sensor and set of coil packs in place of the traditional coil and distributor ignition system. The 1.4-litre CVH engine was reused, and the diesel had grown to 1,753 cc and gained 6 bhp. All petrol units were now able to run on the increasingly widespread, and less harmful, lead-free fuels. The CTX transmission was still available but had undergone an extensive refresh at the Bordeaux transmission plant. Suspension-wise the Fiesta had been re-engineered; the MacPherson strut lower arm mountings were modified for better insulation but increased feel, and the rear beam axle was replaced by a semi-independent torsion beam system allowing a degree of twisting as each trailing arm moved up or down. The new Fiesta was one of the first small cars with optional anti-lock brakes. Derived from the system available on the Escort, the Lucas-Girling mechanical Skid Control System (SCS) genuinely offered a previously unknown level of safety. Another option was the Pilkington 'Quickclear' electrically heated front windscreen, first seen on the 1985 Granada.

On 1 January 1993, the catalytic converter was to become a mandatory fit for petrol engine cars sold in the European Union (in certain US states it had been since the mid-1970s). Fitted into the exhaust manifold to process toxic gases into less harmful emissions, the catalytic converter required very exact fuel control, necessitating a fuel injection system rather than the relatively imprecise and wear-prone carburettor. Fuel injection offers the driver an additional benefit apart from the reduction of emissions; starting the engine at any temperature is reliable and much simplified because the choke control, whether manual and requiring experience and dexterity to adjust, or the often troublesome automatic version, is eliminated with starting, whether from stone cold or after a brief stop on a blisteringly hot day, being managed electronically. By 1990, the Fiesta 1.4 CVH engine, with the still optional catalytic converter, appeared as the 1.4 CFi 'Catalyst', indicating it also had fuel injection. By the start of the following year, all petrol engines could be similarly specified, and gained the CFi tag in place of either CVH or HCS. Things were simpler in 1992 when, in preparation for the regulation, all petrol units moved over to CFi units.

A minor facelift was carried out in 1994 and included engineering and safety improvements such as an even stiffer bodyshell, side-impact beams, seat belt

Above: In line with most of its competitors, five doors were at last available on the third generation Fiesta. This is the 1.1-litre Popular Plus and, while some details were not fitted to the model, thankfully it was bestowed with the very useful heated rear window and rear wash-wipe. (Ford)

Right: The interior of a third generation, three-door, 1.0-litre Popular Plus. Despite languishing towards the bottom of the range, it was nicely finished with most of the features a modern motorist, let alone one from over thirty years ago, would expect. (www.retro-rides.org)

pre-tensioners, suspension revisions along with airbags and optional power steering (essential with the heavier diesel). With an increase in car theft, immobilisers also became standard fit across all UK Fords. With the introduction of a new Fiesta in October 1995, the third generation lived on for a couple more years as the 'Classic'. With the option of the 1.1 or 1.3 CFi (both OHV) petrol or the 1.8 diesel, the Classic was a budget model with a low insurance group rating and, with an attractive Ford financial package, it became a popular first car.

In 1992, Ford dabbled with a three-cylinder, two-stroke engine made by the Australian company Orbital. East German Trabants were smokey and noisy, yet following much development, the Fiesta issued not a single phut-phut. Despite weight and power delivery advantages, undocumented problems encountered during trials – by the Suffolk Constabulary in some cases – led to its cancellation. (Ford)

Fourth Generation (1995–2002)

The BE91 – the codename for the fourth generation Fiesta – was launched in the autumn of 1995. As *Autocar* pointed out, it wasn't a new car but a heavily reworked version of the previous one and, despite looking similar, none of the now slightly more rounded panels were shared. The magazine was impressed with the 1.25-litre version they tested and despite now being one of the more cramped small cars, it was one of the best. With its revised suspension and an all-new engine, *Autocar* said it had 'superb steering and a balance and agility that meant serious driving pleasure was now a reality'.

It's easy to dismiss those suspension revisions as marketing hyperbole but it was part of a sea-change at Ford. As the former group vice-chairman of global product development, Richard Parry-Jones had a distinguished forty-year career during which time he left an indelible mark on the company's products. Parry-Jones brought a much higher standard of vehicle dynamics and sheer driving fun to Ford's European models starting with the Mondeo in 1993, and the Focus five years later. His influence rubbed off on all models including this and every subsequent generation of the Fiesta which were considered among the best handling in their class. Parry-Jones retired from Ford in 2007, but died in an accident involving a tractor on private land near his home at Barmouth in Wales on 16 April 2021 at the age of 69. Despite the loss, the impact of this automotive genius continues to be felt.

The fourth generation Fiesta was simply a heavily revised version of the previous with less angular features and a new fascia. It did, however, get a new, all-alloy, DOHC engine plus truly revolutionary suspension and steering improvements from the maestro that was Richard Parry-Jones. This is a Ghia version with a love-it-or-loathe-it chrome effect grille surround. (Ford)

At least from the rear one can't see the rather awkward grille on the fourth generation Fiesta. Not much has changed but things have got a little more rounded – rather like its Escort and Mondeo stablemates. (Author)

Apart from the old 1.3 CFi Valencia entry-level petrol engine (now renamed Endura-E) and the 1.8-litre diesel carried over from the previous model, the new 1.25-litre unit hailed by *Autocar* was indeed a peach. The CVH had been replaced by an all-aluminium, sixteen-valve double-overhead camshaft engine with multi-point, electronic fuel injection, similar (but not identical) to that first seen in the Mondeo. Called the Zetec-SE, early prototypes were designed and built by Yamaha in Japan before being transferred to Ford's advanced engineering division for completion. Yamaha were considered experts in modern multi-valve technology and had worked as consultants to various European manufacturers. A saving in weight of nearly half when compared with the CVH was achieved not only by the alloy head and block, but also a plastic inlet manifold and a magnesium alloy cam cover. Initially available in 74 bhp 1,242 cc and 89 bhp 1,388 cc versions, production of the smoother, higher-revving engines started on 5 May 1995 at a new £380 million extension to the existing Valencia factory in Spain. The completely revised interior was also praised by *Autocar*, having 'supremely comfortable and supportive seats, clear instruments and neat switchgear'. It had an 'awkward' nose – an oval grille escutcheon – which proved less than popular, and with a chrome finish on Ghia, its ungainliness was even further enhanced; in the light of everything else, however, it was forgiven.

The year 1996 was a record-breaking one for Ford. On 8 October, the British boxer Frank Bruno (1995 World Boxing Council heavyweight champion) drove the 10 millionth Dagenham-built car off the line (a 1.4 Fiesta Ghia) and, with immaculate timing, it was also the 250 millionth vehicle built by Ford *worldwide*. Nine weeks later, the plant built its 29 millionth engine since production began sixty-five years previously.

Daisy, this much-loved 2008 Ford Ka Studio, belongs to Shihanki Elpitiya. Unveiled in 1996, based on the third generation Fiesta and built in Valencia, the fun-to-drive Ka was the perfect modern Mini. Daisy has the updated OHC Duratec engine which replaced the ageing Endura-E OHV unit in 2002 (both displaced 1.3 litres). (Author)

The Ka was designed to attract younger drivers and its large, plastic bumpers meant repair costs – and hence insurance premiums – were kept to a minimum. The interior of the Ka was similarly neat and practical but stylish and appealing. (Ford)

In October 1999, the fourth generation of Fiesta received a minor facelift (the erroneous Mk5) which included a subtle restyle to echo (rather than fully embrace) the 'New Edge' designs of the sub-supermini Ka and the Escort-sized Focus. A design language used by Ford for several products in the late 1990s and early 2000s, the aim of New Edge was to 'distinctly combine intersecting arcs and add creases to soft aerodynamic shapes'. It also meant the loss of the controversial nose and, with restyled wings, a lower bonnet and trapezoidal headlight units which flanked a simple mesh grille, the Fiesta had been transformed once again – although nothing could be done to increase passenger space. In late 2000, the Ghia received a performance boost when its 1.4-litre engine was replaced by the 100 bhp 1.6-litre engine from the sporty Zetec S model, and power steering was fitted to all but the base versions. Limited editions still flourished at Ford and in 2001, two run-out models were produced: the Fun and the Black; apart from the obvious colour of the latter, they gained better trim and included features such as a CD player and air conditioning.

Production of cars finally ended at Dagenham on 20 February 2002; the last to be built was a facelifted, fourth generation Fiesta.

The last car to be built at Dagenham was a fourth generation Ford Fiesta complete with facelift and a new grille. Bringing an end to car production after seventy-one years at the firm's flagship UK plant, it rolled off the line on 20 February 2002 and was signed by anyone and everyone concerned with car. (Author)

The dashboard of the fourth generation Fiesta was totally different to that of the previous and shadowed that in the Escort and Mondeo, but it had lost the open and airy feel. The car acquired a few more features (electric windows, air conditioning, and so on) but the fascia didn't receive much praise. (Ford)

In 1997, a fun-to-drive, three-door coupé based on the fourth generation Fiesta was launched. Named Puma, it had a 1.4- or 1.6-litre Fiesta engine, or the model specific 123 bhp 1.7-litre variable-valve timing engine co-developed with Yamaha. A limited run of 500 'Racing' versions was also available with flared arches and an additional 30 bhp. (Author)

8

Fiesta in the Twenty-First Century

After nearly a quarter of a century of the Fiesta across four versions, Ford knew that to stay towards the top of the sales charts, it was time not just for another revamp, but a major change. The car-buying public was wanting more and more for their money with an increasing level of performance, safety, comfort and convenience. Ford understood this and already had something in the pipeline that would hopefully satisfy many of the needs of the customers of the new millennium.

Fifth Generation (2002–08)

The fifth generation of Fiesta was announced at the Frankfurt Motor Show in September 2001. Launched the following April but initially only in five-door form (codenamed BE256), the new car was totally different; it was tall and spacious, with a set of engines promising economy to lead the field. Feedback from existing owners indicated that a 'big car' premium feel was wanted; it needed to be more refined and comfortable yet still be as cost-effective to run as the best supermini. At the time, it was this generation of Fiesta that represented the single biggest advancement in the history of this model line, and it was also the first to be sold in Asia and Australasia.

The fifth generation of the Fiesta was another all-new model. It was taller and more spacious than before and had a 'big car' feel. This is Jill Smerdon's 2003 five-door 1.25-litre LX finished in Metropolis Blue. (Author)

The soft curves of the old model were replaced by a more modern angular look, using the 'New Edge' style Ford had applied to its other models including the recently updated Mondeo (and partly to the previous generation's facelift). The platform for the new car was shared with Mazda 2; the 121 before it had been practically identical to the previous Fiesta and, for Europe, it was built at Valencia. Ford had a long association with the Japanese brand dating back to 1974, and owned a third of Mazda in 1995 but, following the worldwide recession of the mid-2000s, Ford began to sell off its shares which dropped to 2.1 per cent in 2014, and were fully divested by the end of the following year.

At the lower end of the range, the OHV 1.3L engine (which was initially still available in the UK) was replaced with a 67 bhp 'Rocam' 1,299 cc OHC unit; Rocam was a cost-effective version of the Zetec engine built by Ford of Brazil and renamed 'Duratec'. An updated version of both the 1.25- and 1.4-litre sixteen-valve petrol were available (also renamed Duratec because Zetec was now established as the name of a trim level), and there were a pair of new turbocharged diesels to replace the old and underpowered 1.8-litre normally aspirated unit. The new common-rail 1,398 cc sixteen-valve diesel engine with 67 bhp was a joint development project between Ford and PSA (Peugeot and Citroën). Ford named their version of the engine the 'Duratorq' and gave models with it the designation of TDCi, and

With functional good looks and a usable load space, the fifth generation was, and remains, a great workhorse. Sadly, this version of the small Ford was the first not to be built at Dagenham. From 2002, production of the Fiesta was split between Valencia and Cologne. (Author)

In contrast to the gloom of the fourth generation, the interior of the fifth returned to an open and airy space with all the usual features and fittings expected from a Ford. (Author)

Badged as a Duratec, what nestles beneath the expanse of the plastic engine cover is the 1.25-litre, sixteen-valve, double-overhead camshaft, all-alloy engine first seen in the previous generation Fiesta, and at one time called 'Zetec'. (Author)

The 2002 Ford Fusion was a longer, wider and taller fifth generation Fiesta. Seating five (plus picnic), it had aspects of the Multi-Purpose Vehicle (MPV) and Sport Utility Vehicle (SUV) but without the bulk. Built in Cologne, Ford marketed the vehicle as an 'Urban Activity Vehicle', which 'fused small hatchback, MPV and SUV features together'. (Ford)

within a few months, a 90 bhp 1,560 cc version became available. In mid-November 2002, the range was completed when the three-door Fiesta (the BE257) joined the line-up.

The model received a minor (simply cosmetic) facelift in 2005 when the grille, headlamps and rear lights were tweaked, and the quality of some of the interior trim was improved along with a boost in the radio and related equipment.

Sixth Generation (2008–16)

The sixth generation Fiesta (the B299), with cues from the Verve concept car with its long roof and sculpted body panels, was first unveiled at the Frankfurt Motor Show in September 2007 before its formal launch the following year. Ford described the styling as 'Kinetic Design' and that it was the reason why its vehicles looked more exciting than ever before. The European cars were produced in Cologne and Valencia, but the car was also built for other markets in China, Thailand, Brazil, Mexico and (briefly) the US. As a

In 2008, the sixth generation was unveiled. Another all-new car, Ford suggested it was 'more exciting' than before. The best-selling UK car in every year it was produced, the bang-up-to-date new Fiesta was a revelation. This 2010 1.25-litre Fiesta Zetec finished in Hot Magenta is owned by François Prins. (Prins)

logical subsequent step to that instigated by Ford of Europe back in the 1960s, the model was launched under the company's 'One Ford' strategy which called for single models to be manufactured and sold globally, achieving efficiency and economies of scale.

In B299, Ford had once again produced a new Fiesta with major improvements over the previous version which ensured it stayed at the top of the charts. In the UK, it was the best-selling car in every full year it was produced and 300,000 were sold every year in Europe alone. Across several models from the base Studio to the top Titanium, the Fiesta now had an up-to-date entertainment system ('laid out like a mobile phone', Ford said) with Bluetooth, aux-in and USB connectivity, as well as a radio and CD player. The quality and comfort of the interior also came in for much praise and there was room for five adults, although the rear seat was 'a little tight for three', reported *Autocar*. With a multitude of trim levels and mechanical specifications, there was a Fiesta to suit everyone.

The Duratorq TDCi diesels and the 1.25 and 1.4 petrol units (the smaller being available in two power levels of 60 and 82 bhp) had been carried over, and a new 118 bhp 1.6-litre

Ford said the centre 'hub' of the sixth generation Fiesta fascia was styled along the lines of a mobile phone. This one is colour-coded to blend in nicely with the trim and paint. Note the features: centre display, heated windscreen, air conditioning, Bluetooth, aux-in and a five-speed gearbox. (Prins)

Ford called the styling of the sixth generation 'Kinetic', and it certainly was a change from the previous model. This car looks like it may have aftermarket reversing sensors. (Prins)

The Duratec (previously Zetec) engine in all its glory. To save cost, the engine cover has gone, and the unit is now largely visible. Within a couple of years, the three-cylinder, variable-boost turbocharged, 1.0-litre EcoBoost motor would become available which transformed both power and economy. (Prins)

(1,596 cc) 'Twin independent Variable Camshaft Timing' (Ti-VCT) petrol engine had been added. Ford had already introduced 'ECOnetic' as a general technology on other models to reduce emissions and improve fuel economy and, in 2009, the Fiesta version was available. The main feature of ECOnetic was a 1.6-litre diesel engine tuned for efficiency and the brochure promised 'up to' 78.5 mpg. A feature called 'Easy Fuel' had also been added to all variants which removed the need for a separate cap beneath the fuel flap, and a device in the filler neck prevented both wrong fuel being used as well as theft by siphoning. The overall safety of the Fiesta was not forgotten with Ford's 'Intelligent Protection System' or IPS, which included passive safety features such as a cabin safety cell, and active ones such as electronic stability control, seat belt pre-tensioners and 'Active City Stop' which applied the brakes if sensors at the front detected an imminent crash.

In 2012, the engine range was dramatically revised with the inclusion of the 1.0-litre three-cylinder 'EcoBoost' unit used to great acclaim in the Focus. Codenamed Fox and designed by engineers at Dunton, its diminutive footprint belied the sophistication of the engine (it was compared to A4 paper size – about 300 × 210 mm). With variable valve timing, direct injection, a variable boost turbocharger and a new six-speed gearbox, the triple produced smooth, refined power with low emissions and a level of torque usually associated with at least 1.6 litres. Losing a cylinder not only sheds weight (30 kg) but frictional losses are reduced and, with the other features, the Fiesta was capable of 65 mpg. Despite displacing less than the older engines, sophistication is expensive so a budget 1.25 petrol and the diesel were still available.

EcoBoost was so good it picked up a series of awards. In 2012, it won three from the International Engine of the Year committee for Best New Engine, Best Overall Engine (repeated the following two years) and Best Up To 1.0 litre (reprised annually up to and including 2017); in 2019, it was judged the Best Up To 150 PS (metric horsepower or 148 bhp). No other unit has won as many awards from this panel, or won them across such a long period. In 2013, the 1.0-litre EcoBoost Fiesta was voted the Women's World Car of the Year, when a panel of eighteen female motoring writers chose the car for its value-for-money, appearance, storage, child-friendliness and limited environmental footprint.

In 2012, production of the Fiesta ceased at Valencia, and the line was transferred to the only remaining European facility for the small car at Cologne (since its transfer from Saarlouis in 1980). Two years later, the Fiesta became the best-selling car ever in the UK when it surpassed the 4.1 million total of its (by then obsolete) sibling, the Ford Escort.

Seventh Generation (2016–23)

It was difficult to imagine how the sixth generation Fiesta could be improved, but an update was due and, in 2016, the new Fiesta (codenamed B479) was launched. Despite any similarity to the previous, the seventh generation was completely new. It was now a safer, roomier car with modern technology equal to the best of its competitors; it had an 8-inch central screen, digital radio, the option of a Bang & Olufsen premium sound system and enhanced safety features to both alert the driver and steer the car back on course when the car strayed over a white line, or another vehicle had strayed into a blind spot. A premium Vignale version (described by Ford as 'a world of contemporary luxury') with yet more standard features created a large car feel in a small package and, with the optional 'Active Park Assist', it could even park itself! With its combination of performance, handling, features and comfort, the motoring press ranked the new Fiesta as one of the best – if not *the* best – in its class.

The 1.0-litre three-cylinder EcoBoost engines with 100, 125 or 140 PS remained, although a more affordable Fiesta (with a lower insurance rating) was also available in the form of a 1.1-litre non-turbocharged three-cylinder 'Ti-VCT' engine with either 70 or 85 bhp. Cylinder deactivation technology also became available on the EcoBoost which stopped fuel and valve operation for the middle cylinder when not needed (coasting or light-throttle cruising) and, with the on or off process taking just 14 milliseconds, it was all but imperceptible to the driver and it was a world first for a triple.

A minor facelift was applied in 2021 comprising a new grille with the option of adaptive LED matrix headlights, a bigger 12.3-inch digital dashboard and the availability of a seven-speed 'Powershift' automatic transmission. In 2019, just 2 per cent of Fiesta sales in the UK were diesels, and in line with environmental concerns, the option was dropped. A mild-hybrid EcoBoost petrol engine (badged mHEV) effectively replaced the diesel unit and, with a 153 bhp option, it offered low emissions coupled with excellent performance.

The seventh generation of the Ford Fiesta was the last to be produced and, in the summer of 2023, production at Cologne stopped.

Above: At a few paces, the seventh generation of 2016 looked very similar to the previous, but it was actually completely new. It was safer, roomier and had a level of technology and features by then expected on any car, even the smaller models. This one is a 2019 Titanium model finished in Chrome Blue, and it belongs to Jonathan Wankling. (Author)

Below: Also a seventh generation, this is Julie Smith's three-door ST-Line model finished in Blue Wave, and is fitted with the 125PS (123 bhp) EcoBoost engine. ST-line meant sporty by nature but not expense. (Author)

The three-cylinder, 1.0-litre 100PS (98 bhp) EcoBoost engine in Jonathan's 2019 Titanium. The three coil packs and the Lambda mixture sensor can clearly be seen amongst the plethora of cables and pipes. (Author)

The interior of the seventh generation Fiesta really was fully equipped and very modern. A large screen dominates the centre, and it is equipped with virtually every technological feature expected of any car of the late 2010s. This particular car is an automatic. (Author)

In 2017 and in an attempt to jump on the bottom end of the SUV market, Ford unveiled the Fiesta Active. Based on the seventh generation Fiesta with raised suspension (by 18 mm), plastic wheel arch extensions, roof bars and a choice of EcoBoost triples, reports referred to it as 'An appealing and likeable small SUV'. (Author)

9

Some Like it Hot

As the 1960s dawned, Ford had become aware of the performance image which wooed the younger car buyer and, having dismissed the idea of an outright sports car with its limited market potential, it needed something else with a similar draw. An added incentive came in the form of the BMC Mini Cooper which, with its competition success and the resulting publicity, proved that a standard production car could be transformed into something with sporting potential. Roll on another fifteen years and, after the successes of the Cortina (both the developed-by-Lotus version and Ford's own GT) and a bevy of performance Escorts, it was inevitable that the company's smallest car would receive similar treatment.

In 1979, Donald Healey (of Austin-Healey) was commissioned to build a Healey Fiesta concept based on a tuned Federal Fiesta, and fitted with flared arches, alloys and square headlamps. Finished in British Racing Green with yards of yellow coachlines, only one was built, although an unofficial replica has since been constructed. (Graham Robson Collection)

Starting Point

The 1100S of 1976 was the first sporty Fiesta. The model was fun to drive yet even with the performance boost of the 1300 version just over a year later, a zero to 60 mph time of just under 12 seconds meant the car was lively but not fast. What these models did achieve, however, was the acceptance of a sports Fiesta and in 1981, the limited edition 1300S-based 'Supersport' certainly looked the part and would pave the way for the forthcoming XR2. With a run of 3,000, it was available in black, white, silver or red with black polyurethane arch extensions over 6 × 13-inch RS alloy wheels (Rallye Sport, a Ford sub-brand dating back to 1967), complete with a small bulge in the rear valence to accommodate the spare. Topped off with a front air dam, bootlid spoiler, driving lamps, body-coloured grille and decals, it was the input of Ford's Special Vehicle Engineering team at Dunton (SVE) that gave the model its credibility; an association that for anything Ford and sporty, was set to last. The brochure suggested the Supersport would provide 'the affordable alternative to mundane motoring', and as such it was a relatively early contender in the emerging hot hatch craze of the 1980s.

The 1.1-litre first generation S was the first sporty Fiesta, soon followed by a 1.3-litre version. Striped seats, 'S' decals ('1300S' on the bigger-engined version), sports suspension and a tachometer made the S the one the keener driver lusted after. The head restraints and alloy wheels on this one were optional extras. (Ford)

All 3,000 of the limited edition Supersport (based on the 1300S) were fully bedecked in broad side stripes, wide alloy wheels with plastic arches, driving lamps and 'special' seats with head restraints. It was a trial run for the planned XR2 and Ford's advertising people didn't play down the performance and handling either... (Ford)

XR2

There remains speculation about the meaning of 'XR' (Xtra Rally or Experimental Racing) but for Ford it was an important tag for their higher performance models. Following the Escort XR3 of 1980, the Fiesta XR2 appeared a few months later based on a 1.6-litre Kent-powered North American version uprated to a more healthy 84 bhp. With the circular Federal headlights plus decals, spoilers, arches, stiffer springing and Wolfrace Sonic alloy wheels, 60 was dispatched in 9.3 seconds – 'Highly tuned but not highly strung', Ford said. The XR2 was available with various options including the 'Climate Control Pack' comprising all-round tinted glass with a darker band at the top of the windscreen, and front opening quarter windows – an air-conditioned Fiesta was still several years away for markets other than North America. The XR2 was certainly successful; at its peak, it accounted for 25 per cent of Fiesta sales and the model was more profitable than a 1.1L (the most popular trim level). After barely three years, however, the second generation XR2 appeared. It had lost its decals but gained refinement and a little performance with the 96 bhp 1.6-litre CVH engine and five-speed gearbox from the XR3.

Left: An amalgam of the Supersport and the US 'Federal' specification Fiesta with the latter's circular headlamps and 1.6-litre engine, the first XR2 was a pocket rocket – or that's what some of the testers suggested. One wonders what the buyers of the (1.3-litre) Supersport said when Ford unveiled this (faster and better equipped) model just a few months later. (Ford)

Below: There's no doubt that Ford hit the spot with the XR2. It's a perfect manifestation of a Mini Cooper for the 1980s, but it's much better in so many ways and it's more practical. You could commute in it, go shopping in it, take your friends out and generally have fun with it. (Ford)

This new owner looks a little smug with her XR2, and who can blame her? She also doesn't seem too upset about the peculiar lack of (the supposedly standard fitment) driving lamps – maybe it's just an oversight despite Ford giving you more. (Ford)

Above left: Studio lighting accepted, the interior of the first XR2 was comfortable and well equipped. Ford's styling and marketing departments had got so much so right: the roof-mounted LCD clock, the push-button radio, the larger gear knob, the chunky steering wheel, not to mention the superbly supportive seats. (Ford)

Above right: Did we mention the stripes, plastic arches and the wide, low-profile tyres wrapping the alloy wheels on the first generation XR2? (Ford)

The second generation XR2 gained the 1.6-litre CVH engine from the XR3 and was basically a more refined and developed version of the very successful but quite short-lived first incarnation. With sporty, chunky good looks coupled with respectable performance and handling, the XR2 remains sought-after today. (Ford)

The interior of the second generation XR2. It was very successful the first time around, so the theme was repeated: additional instrumentation, special steering wheel and bucket-style seats. (Author)

Fuel Injection and Turbocharging

Following the success of the XR2 package, it was inevitable that performance models of the new third generation Fiesta would also be offered, and customers weren't disappointed. A mildly sporting 90 bhp 1.6S CVH model was available from launch but, in August 1989, a new XR2i was launched with (optional) Recaro seats, special alloy wheels and a quartet of spot and fog lamps in the bumper to set it apart from its lesser siblings. The 'i' suffix meant fuel injection (the first petrol Fiesta without a carburettor) and, for the first two years, the XR2i had the injected 110 bhp 1.6-litre CVH engine (1,597 cc) from the XR3i, although in practice its performance wasn't dramatically better than the previous model. A more expensive, higher performance version was offered a few months later alongside the XR2i in the form of the RS Turbo and, with 133 bhp, 60 appeared in 7.9 seconds. The Garrett TO2 turbocharger bolted to the CVH unit provided an abundance of torque with 135 lb ft available from 2,400 rpm right up to 5,000, meaning cross-country and passing times were very impressive – although Ford did have to strengthen the five-speed gearbox to cope. Visually similar to the XR2i, the Spanish-built RS Turbo had larger (by 1 inch) diameter 14-inch alloys of a different design and a green stripe instead of blue. It also gained RS bonnet louvres, opening rear windows, a leather-clad three-spoke steering wheel and 'Benetton' velour fabric-trimmed Recaros. Whilst the forced-induction variant was quick,

Above: This is a third generation, three-door 1.6S – a warm rather than a hot hatch. Intended for owners unable to finance, insure or just not needing the performance advantage of the XR2i, this model was still sporty and a pleasure to drive. Despite around 20 bhp less than its bigger brother, it was barely a second slower to 60, cheaper to run and much more likely to still be where one parked it. (Ford)

Left: With the drivers of fast Fords no doubt being partial to a spicy meal from an Indian subcontinent-themed eating establishment, the advertising department at Ford thought rather than bamboozle potential customers with figures and specifications, relate the top two performing Fiestas to their favourite curries. Naturally, the RS Turbo is the hottest of the two. (Ford)

Above: So similar are the RS1800 and the XR2i, it's difficult to tell them apart, but the blue car is the former and the red one the latter. As the RS1800 overtook your XR2i (as it inevitably would), you'd probably miss the extra slits in the five-spoke 14-inch alloys. What you might spot, though, is the RS1800 badge on the boot lid as it disappeared off up the road. (Ford)

Below: Single-make racing relies on the skill of the drivers and teams in their matched cars. Oulton Park, 10 September 1995: John Bintcliffe leads at Cascades Corner, with Gary Burridge and Mike Gorton chasing. Competing in the Ford Credit Fiesta Challenge, they are all equipped with RS1800s. John won the race (and £450) and went on to win the championship (£6,000). (Steve Martin/Ford)

it acquired a reputation for lacking smoothness with its significant turbo lag and torque steer; *Autocar* went a little further and described it as 'uncouth'.

With the imminent phasing out of the CVH engine but also to address the day-to-day living issues with the RS Turbo, in 1992 the XR2i gained a new engine. The updated car was basically unchanged but now had a smoother and more refined 1.8-litre sixteen-valve DOHC unit with 105 bhp. Initially called Zeta, Lancia already owned the trademark and threatened legal action so Ford named its engine 'Zetec'. With Recaro seats, five-spoke alloys, a spoiler and despite the similar performance to its predecessor, the new XR2i was clearly in a different class. A replacement for the RS Turbo was also offered and the RS 1800 (its name alone harking back to the rally-bred 1970s Escort Mk2) had a similar 1,796 cc Zetec but tuned for an extra 23 bhp, with the result that 60 came up in 8.3 seconds. Whilst not as fast in outright figures as the turbocharged car, it was less brutal and much easier to live with, although the better handling (so the various tests reported) Renault Clio 16v at £12,337 was £500 cheaper.

Six Group 2 Fiesta 1600S rally cars were built and debuted at the 1979 Monte Carlo. Ari Vatanen and David Richards finished tenth, with Roger Clark and Jim Porter three places behind. This car was reserved for the Roger Clark Fiesta training programme but, having never been used, it was sold off. It has since been restored as a faithful replica of Clark's Monte car. (Graham Robson Collection)

Joy Riding

As cars became more and more desirable, but with their locks and security systems having stagnated technically for a decade or more, vehicle theft became more prevalent. The economic situation of the day doubtless didn't help but 'joy riding' (where cars are stolen and driven recklessly, often to destruction) had become a major nuisance in the latter half of the 1980s and for the owner it was anything but a joy. Insurance companies started to refuse to cover certain models – including the various performance-oriented Fords – or they quoted unreasonable premiums often above the value of the car. Manufacturers had to do something to reduce the risk; it wasn't all down to struggling law enforcement. New models came out with engine immobilisers, alarms, coded radios and door locks with deadbolts – Ford changed to Chubb (and later Tibbe) locks which were considered less easy to pick. Some companies produced insurance-friendly sporty models which were less attractive to criminals and one of the first was the third-generation Ford Fiesta Si. With a 90 bhp 1.6-litre 16V Zetec and less overtly performance-oriented advertising, the relatively standard-looking Si could reach 60 in 10.1 seconds, so in everyday driving it was not a lot slower than the costlier to buy and far harder to insure XR2i. By the turn of the millennium, with the theft and insurance problems largely overcome and the XR2i along with the RS Turbo and 1800 almost forgotten, it was time to create a proper sporty Fiesta again!

The ST Factor

There had been a fourth generation Fiesta (the facelifted version of 1999) with the model designation Zetec S and a 1.6-litre 100 bhp DOHC engine but, despite its neat and accomplished handling, its mediocre specification meant it languished in the shadow of its XR and RS predecessors. When the new Fiesta appeared in 2002, however, it was time for a change and Ford's Team RS organisation (replacing SVE) had already come up with ST, or 'Sports Technologies', to indicate the high-performance version of various Ford models.

The first Fiesta ST was unveiled at the Geneva Motor Show in March 2004 and it went on sale in the UK the following winter. Based on the fifth generation and weighing just over 1,000 kg, its 2.0-litre 148 bhp DOHC Duratec (Zetec-derived) sixteen-valve engine meant it could reach 60 in 7.9 seconds with handling to match. Unofficially referred to as the ST150 (its power in PS), it was the first Fiesta to be fitted with rear discs, and the option list included full leather and lower side stripes. Ford also offered a couple of official performance upgrades to either 165 or 185 bhp, although even in standard form the ST was fun and affordable, with a decent set of sporting accoutrements. The UK-only limited edition ST500 of April 2008 was only available in black and it didn't have any engine upgrades, but it did gain heated leather, red brake callipers, 17-inch wheels and special silver decals including a U-shaped sticker on the bonnet. The fifth generation Fiesta was discontinued in 2008 but the ST story wasn't going to stop there!

The first ST was based on the fifth generation Fiesta with a 148 bhp, 2.0-litre DOHC Duratec. Note the deeper front air dam and the low-profile tyres. With 60 appearing in a shade under 8 seconds, it didn't disgrace itself. (Ford)

The interior of the ST was inspiring too, and the super supportive seats helped make the driver and their passenger feel they were in something fairly special. Note the appropriate logos on the seat backs. (Ford)

With the launch of the sixth generation Fiesta, enthusiasts had to make do at first with another 'warm' Zetec S model, fitted with either a 1.6-litre Ti-VCT petrol or even the TDCi diesel. Nearly five years on, however, and with experience gained from the new Focus ST, the second Fiesta ST was unveiled in March 2013. Fitted with an all-alloy four-cylinder 1,596 cc 1.6-litre EcoBoost engine having all the usual features of the technology by then already available in three-cylinder 1.0-litre form on the 'standard' Fiestas (including turbocharging and variable valve timing) resulted in 179 bhp, meaning 60 appeared in just 6.8 seconds. With its tenacious handling, it was *the* small hot hatch to have – particularly at just £16,995 which undercut its similarly performing rival, the Renault Clio RS220, by nearly £5,000. The unit wasn't short of torque either with 199 lb ft spread evenly from 1,900 to 4,000 rpm, blessing the ST with a very wide spread of performance for such a modest capacity right up to a maximum speed of 139 mph. With full throttle and either third or fourth gear selected, 'overboost' was applied which, by varying the vanes in the turbocharger and raising the waste gate limit, provided around 10 per cent extra power for 10 seconds. The ST didn't have a limited-slip differential (LSD) but it did have 'Torque Vectoring Control' which applied the brake to an inside spinning front wheel to regain traction. Three trim levels of ST were available, ST-1, ST-2 and (later) ST-3, each having ascending levels of features and equipment. The Fiesta ST was receiving praise from far and wide, and the magazine partner of the popular BBC TV motoring show *Top Gear* chose the ST as its 2013 Car of the Year.

The Finnish combo of Mikko Hirvonen and Jarmo Lehtinen in a Ford Fiesta World Rally Championship (WRC) RS on their way to an outright win in the 2011 Rally of Sweden. That same year, Hirvonen went on to finish as runner-up in the WRC to Frenchman and nine-time championship winner Sébastien Loeb. (Graham Robson Collection)

As part of the 2015 refresh of the Ford Motor Company's high-performance sector, Ford Performance was devised. Formally Ford Racing, the new division was the label attached to its motor sport and racing activities – including certain road cars – and the Fiesta ST was deemed a worthy recipient of the tag. One of the first projects for Ford Performance was a run-out limited edition model for 2016, the ST200, based on the ST-3 and built to celebrate forty years of the Fiesta. With a price premium of nearly £3,000, the limited edition was only available in light Storm Grey but it had matching Recaros plus revised springs, dampers, front anti-roll bar and rear torsion beam. An additional 5 seconds of overboost meant the ST200 was slightly faster, and its suspension modifications meant it was better riding than the standard ST, but it could still top 50 mpg and its handling remained impeccable. Much to some ST200 buyers' chagrin, within a matter of months all ST models received similar modifications at no extra cost. In 2016, Team RS created ST-Line, a trim level designation having some of the sporty nature of ST such as lower and stiffer suspension, more supportive seats, improved equipment and little more power, but without the extreme performance and higher running costs (such as insurance) of its ST stablemate.

The limited edition ST200 of 2016 celebrated forty years of the Fiesta. Based on the sixth generation Fiesta ST-3 with the four-cylinder, 1.6-litre EcoBoost engine, but with an additional 5 seconds of overboost, 60 was reached in under 7 seconds. (Author)

This is Martin Hermes' 2020 seventh generation Fiesta ST-3 finished in Performance Blue and fitted with the Performance Pack which includes a Quaife differential. Note also the 18-inch alloys and red brake callipers. The branded mudflaps and rear number plate surround are aftermarket additions. (Author)

With the seventh generation of Ford Fiesta, the third (and what became the final) ST was unveiled in 2018, along with mildly sporty 1.0-litre ST-Line models. Whilst still fitted with an EcoBoost under the bonnet, the ST now used the slightly smaller all-alloy 1.5-litre 1,497 cc unit with just three cylinders (codenamed Dragon) and was the first Ford Performance model to be powered by a triple. One or two motoring journalists were concerned that the deletion of a cylinder and the loss of 100 cc might have affected performance, but they needn't have worried. With 197 bhp and 214 lb ft of torque (spread slightly wider than before from 1,600 to 4,000 rpm) and similar overboost features as before, the new ST was slightly faster than the 1.6 with 60 arriving in 6.6 seconds before going on to a possible 144 mph, and the torque ensured the ST had retained its impressive mid-range acceleration. The engine also had the middle cylinder deactivation feature from the 1.0 litre which, under light loads, helped it achieve its impressive parsimony.

Not much to see here! Beneath the plastic engine cover of Martin's ST-3 is a 1.5-litre, three-cylinder EcoBoost with 197 bhp and torque to match, meaning 60 appears in less than 7 seconds. It's economical too, giving at least 40 miles per gallon. Note the 'Ford Performance' factory branding. (Author)

The front view of Martin's ST-3. Its very purposeful stance with its serious performance and long list of technological features means it has come a long way from the first generation models. (Author)

On the options list was a 'Performance Pack' for £850 which included quicker steering, launch control and a Quaife-manufactured, limited-slip differential (LSD) to reduce tyre spin – a very likely side-effect of the torque levels available in a relatively light, front-wheel drive car. The standard ST had the torque vectoring system which worked fine in normal driving, but a relatively powerful car being driven enthusiastically benefited from a 'proper' LSD – and it would ease the later homologation process. In ST-3 trim, the car was very well equipped with 18-inch alloys, red brake callipers, part-leather Recaros, a rear-view camera and keyless entry and start. At £21,495 the Fiesta ST-3 seriously undercut its closest rival the Renault Megane RS by over £7,000. As with the previous ST, engine noise was considered important and the 'Sound Symposer' system fed a synthesised sound into the cabin. Depending on the mode selected by the driver (such as eco, normal or track which varied throttle and steering response, as well as stability control intrusion), the exhaust note could be made to crackle and pop on the overrun, just like a rally car...

A minor facelift in 2021 included a five-door option for the ST, a new coarse-mesh grille complete with the blue oval Ford badge moved from the front panel, adaptive LEDs and one or two other bits and pieces before the Fiesta's sad demise just a couple of years later. *Top Gear* magazine rated the Fiesta ST as 'an accessible performance car bargain' and, in 2018, they awarded it Car of the Year for a second time. What a swansong!

10

Legacy

Given the unquestionable ubiquity of the Ford Fiesta, it's hard to believe that, after forty-seven years, production of the model ceased. There is no doubt that when Ford launched the Fiesta in 1976, it set the supermini benchmark for packaging, driving pleasure and ease of ownership by simply doing most things better than its competitors. The Renault 5 had been one of the leaders in the small car sector since its launch in 1971, but the emergence of the Fiesta suddenly made all other competitors – including this one – seem outdated. The Ford may not have had the French car's *joie de vivre*, yet as a sensible, practical, reliable and good-looking hatchback, it won many buyers not just in Britain, but all over Europe and beyond.

When production of the Ford Fiesta ended, it was the UK's best-selling car of all time, with 4.8 million of the total global production of 22 million ending up on the roads of Britain; in 1990, 1991, 1996 to 1998 and then in a twelve-year consecutive run from 2009, the Fiesta was the country's top-seller. It might have been top-of-the-list as a buyers' car, but the Fiesta was equally popular for those keen to acquire an example without having to pay for it. In 2023, the Ford gained a dubious reputation as the most stolen car in Britain. According to *What Car* magazine, 64,087 cars were stolen that year (176 every day, or about one every 8 minutes), and 5,979 of them were Fiestas – that's around sixteen every day. This rather unfortunate score has a lot to do with the popularity of the model: there are millions for both car buyers and thieves to choose from, and rich pickings for either spare parts or complete vehicles.

There are several possible reasons for the 2023 demise of the Fiesta. The profit on a smaller and less expensive car is correspondingly less (mini cars but mini profits, is quoted) but, especially with the increasingly complex and feature-rich modern car, the build costs are not *proportionately* less. Car manufacturers would rather concentrate on larger and higher-specification models with better margins, coinciding neatly with the current fashion for Sports Utility Vehicles (SUVs). The move to the Electric Vehicle (EV) is another reason. With the current battery and motor technologies, building a small EV (such as a Fiesta EV) with the range buyers demand is difficult, even though around 95 per cent of journeys are usually local. Around the time of the loss of the Fiesta, the small car and the EV markets were in a state of confusion; some manufacturers stopped producing such cars, but other manufacturers widened their small car range, managing to increase sales. Ford might not have embarked on the development of an eighth generation of the Fiesta, but the final model may have sold for a couple of years longer. Fortunately for Ford, the 2019 Puma, a sub-compact, crossover SUV based on the floorpan of the out-going Fiesta, has – with the help of enthusiastic sales staff – mopped up a proportion of the small car's sales. These factors led to the drop-off in sales of the Fiesta over the last few years of production, and it simply didn't make business sense for Ford to continue with its manufacture.

Whilst the production numbers and longevity are impressive, it's the car itself that we should celebrate. All seven generations of Fiesta attract a lot of attention. With modest and high-performance models plus virtually everything in between, it has an enduring popularity in both the classic and the modern car arenas. Even now production has ended, the Fiesta continues to provide reliable and cost-effective transport for many people, and the car will doubtless remain a valuable workhorse for several years to come. The Ford Fiesta has been part of so many people's lives, certainly in Britain, that the model is usually considered to be British; they have driven one, owned one, learnt to drive in one, known a friend or relative with one, been a passenger in one or just seen them on the roads and driveways of Britain over many years. It's tempting to describe the Fiesta as dead, but it isn't. Ford retains the rights to the name and perhaps one day it may return, although possibly not in a form we recognise, but for the moment at least: long live the Ford Fiesta!

One of the last two Ford Fiestas to roll off the production line at Cologne on Friday 7 July 2023. Both were signed by all concerned and this shot rather neatly highlights the minor changes introduced by the final facelift to the seventh generation – mainly the grille, its badge and the front lights. (Author)